CS-32   GENERAL APTITUDE AND ABILITIES SERIES

This is your
PASSBOOK for...

Police Administration & Supervision

Test Preparation Study Guide
Questions & Answers

COPYRIGHT NOTICE

This book is SOLELY intended for, is sold ONLY to, and its use is RESTRICTED to individual, bona fide applicants or candidates who qualify by virtue of having seriously filed applications for appropriate license, certificate, professional and/or promotional advancement, higher school matriculation, scholarship, or other legitimate requirements of education and/or governmental authorities.

This book is NOT intended for use, class instruction, tutoring, training, duplication, copying, reprinting, excerption, or adaptation, etc., by:

1) Other publishers
2) Proprietors and/or Instructors of "Coaching" and/or Preparatory Courses
3) Personnel and/or Training Divisions of commercial, industrial, and governmental organizations
4) Schools, colleges, or universities and/or their departments and staffs, including teachers and other personnel
5) Testing Agencies or Bureaus
6) Study groups which seek by the purchase of a single volume to copy and/or duplicate and/or adapt this material for use by the group as a whole without having purchased individual volumes for each of the members of the group
7) Et al.

Such persons would be in violation of appropriate Federal and State statutes.

PROVISION OF LICENSING AGREEMENTS – Recognized educational, commercial, industrial, and governmental institutions and organizations, and others legitimately engaged in educational pursuits, including training, testing, and measurement activities, may address request for a licensing agreement to the copyright owners, who will determine whether, and under what conditions, including fees and charges, the materials in this book may be used them. In other words, a licensing facility exists for the legitimate use of the material in this book on other than an individual basis. However, it is asseverated and affirmed here that the material in this book CANNOT be used without the receipt of the express permission of such a licensing agreement from the Publishers. Inquiries re licensing should be addressed to the company, attention rights and permissions department.

All rights reserved, including the right of reproduction in whole or in part, in any form or by any means, electronic or mechanical, including photocopying, recording, or by any information storage and retrieval system, without permission in writing from the Publisher.

Copyright © 2025 by
National Learning Corporation

212 Michael Drive, Syosset, NY 11791
(516) 921-8888 • www.passbooks.com
E-mail: info@passbooks.com

PASSBOOK® SERIES

THE *PASSBOOK® SERIES* has been created to prepare applicants and candidates for the ultimate academic battlefield – the examination room.

At some time in our lives, each and every one of us may be required to take an examination – for validation, matriculation, admission, qualification, registration, certification, or licensure.

Based on the assumption that every applicant or candidate has met the basic formal educational standards, has taken the required number of courses, and read the necessary texts, the *PASSBOOK® SERIES* furnishes the one special preparation which may assure passing with confidence, instead of failing with insecurity. Examination questions – together with answers – are furnished as the basic vehicle for study so that the mysteries of the examination and its compounding difficulties may be eliminated or diminished by a sure method.

This book is meant to help you pass your examination provided that you qualify and are serious in your objective.

The entire field is reviewed through the huge store of content information which is succinctly presented through a provocative and challenging approach – the question-and-answer method.

A climate of success is established by furnishing the correct answers at the end of each test.

You soon learn to recognize types of questions, forms of questions, and patterns of questioning. You may even begin to anticipate expected outcomes.

You perceive that many questions are repeated or adapted so that you can gain acute insights, which may enable you to score many sure points.

You learn how to confront new questions, or types of questions, and to attack them confidently and work out the correct answers.

You note objectives and emphases, and recognize pitfalls and dangers, so that you may make positive educational adjustments.

Moreover, you are kept fully informed in relation to new concepts, methods, practices, and directions in the field.

You discover that you are actually taking the examination all the time: you are preparing for the examination by "taking" an examination, not by reading extraneous and/or supererogatory textbooks.

In short, this PASSBOOK®, used directedly, should be an important factor in helping you to pass your test.

POLICE ADMINISTRATION & SUPERVISION

The General Aptitude and Abilities Series provides functional, intensive test practice and drill in the basic skills and areas common to many civil service, general aptitude and achievement examinations necessary for entrance into schools or occupations.

Passbooks in this series use a variety of question types, and other applicable items like charts, graphs, illustrations and more, to prepare candidates for testing in particular subject areas. This Passbook features a wide range of questions covering general supervision, police administration and organization; and more.

HOW TO TAKE A TEST

You have studied long, hard and conscientiously.

With your official admission card in hand, and your heart pounding, you have been admitted to the examination room.

You note that there are several hundred other applicants in the examination room waiting to take the same test.

They all appear to be equally well prepared.

You know that nothing but your best effort will suffice. The "moment of truth" is at hand: you now have to demonstrate objectively, in writing, your knowledge of content and your understanding of subject matter.

You are fighting the most important battle of your life—to pass and/or score high on an examination which will determine your career and provide the economic basis for your livelihood.

What extra, special things should you know and should you do in taking the examination?

I. YOU MUST PASS AN EXAMINATION

A. WHAT EVERY CANDIDATE SHOULD KNOW
Examination applicants often ask us for help in preparing for the written test. What can I study in advance? What kinds of questions will be asked? How will the test be given? How will the papers be graded?

B. HOW ARE EXAMS DEVELOPED?
Examinations are carefully written by trained technicians who are specialists in the field known as "psychological measurement," in consultation with recognized authorities in the field of work that the test will cover. These experts recommend the subject matter areas or skills to be tested; only those knowledges or skills important to your success on the job are included. The most reliable books and source materials available are used as references. Together, the experts and technicians judge the difficulty level of the questions.
Test technicians know how to phrase questions so that the problem is clearly stated. Their ethics do not permit "trick" or "catch" questions. Questions may have been tried out on sample groups, or subjected to statistical analysis, to determine their usefulness.
Written tests are often used in combination with performance tests, ratings of training and experience, and oral interviews. All of these measures combine to form the best-known means of finding the right person for the right job.

II. HOW TO PASS THE WRITTEN TEST

A. BASIC STEPS

1) Study the announcement

How, then, can you know what subjects to study? Our best answer is: "Learn as much as possible about the class of positions for which you've applied." The exam will test the knowledge, skills and abilities needed to do the work.

Your most valuable source of information about the position you want is the official exam announcement. This announcement lists the training and experience qualifications. Check these standards and apply only if you come reasonably close to meeting them. Many jurisdictions preview the written test in the exam announcement by including a section called "Knowledge and Abilities Required," "Scope of the Examination," or some similar heading. Here you will find out specifically what fields will be tested.

2) Choose appropriate study materials

If the position for which you are applying is technical or advanced, you will read more advanced, specialized material. If you are already familiar with the basic principles of your field, elementary textbooks would waste your time. Concentrate on advanced textbooks and technical periodicals. Think through the concepts and review difficult problems in your field.

These are all general sources. You can get more ideas on your own initiative, following these leads. For example, training manuals and publications of the government agency which employs workers in your field can be useful, particularly for technical and professional positions. A letter or visit to the government department involved may result in more specific study suggestions, and certainly will provide you with a more definite idea of the exact nature of the position you are seeking.

3) Study this book!

III. KINDS OF TESTS

Tests are used for purposes other than measuring knowledge and ability to perform specified duties. For some positions, it is equally important to test ability to make adjustments to new situations or to profit from training. In others, basic mental abilities not dependent on information are essential. Questions which test these things may not appear as pertinent to the duties of the position as those which test for knowledge and information. Yet they are often highly important parts of a fair examination. For very general questions, it is almost impossible to help you direct your study efforts. What we can do is to point out some of the more common of these general abilities needed in public service positions and describe some typical questions.

1) General information

Broad, general information has been found useful for predicting job success in some kinds of work. This is tested in a variety of ways, from vocabulary lists to questions about current events. Basic background in some field of work, such as sociology or economics, may be sampled in a group of questions. Often these are principles which have become familiar to most persons through exposure rather than through formal training. It is difficult to advise you how to study for these questions; being alert to the world around you is our best suggestion.

2) Verbal ability

An example of an ability needed in many positions is verbal or language ability. Verbal ability is, in brief, the ability to use and understand words. Vocabulary and grammar tests are typical measures of this ability. Reading comprehension or paragraph interpretation questions are common in many kinds of civil service tests. You are given a paragraph of written material and asked to find its central meaning.

IV. KINDS OF QUESTIONS

1. Multiple-choice Questions

Most popular of the short-answer questions is the "multiple choice" or "best answer" question. It can be used, for example, to test for factual knowledge, ability to solve problems or judgment in meeting situations found at work.

A multiple-choice question is normally one of three types:
- It can begin with an incomplete statement followed by several possible endings. You are to find the one ending which best completes the statement, although some of the others may not be entirely wrong.
- It can also be a complete statement in the form of a question which is answered by choosing one of the statements listed.
- It can be in the form of a problem – again you select the best answer.

Here is an example of a multiple-choice question with a discussion which should give you some clues as to the method for choosing the right answer:

When an employee has a complaint about his assignment, the action which will best help him overcome his difficulty is to
    A. discuss his difficulty with his coworkers
    B. take the problem to the head of the organization
    C. take the problem to the person who gave him the assignment
    D. say nothing to anyone about his complaint

In answering this question, you should study each of the choices to find which is best. Consider choice "A" – Certainly an employee may discuss his complaint with fellow employees, but no change or improvement can result, and the complaint remains unresolved. Choice "B" is a poor choice since the head of the organization probably does not know what assignment you have been given, and taking your problem to him is known as "going over the head" of the supervisor. The supervisor, or person who made the assignment, is the person who can clarify it or correct any injustice. Choice "C" is, therefore, correct. To say nothing, as in choice "D," is unwise. Supervisors have and interest in knowing the problems employees are facing, and the employee is seeking a solution to his problem.

2. True/False

3. Matching Questions

Matching an answer from a column of choices within another column.

V. RECORDING YOUR ANSWERS

Computer terminals are used more and more today for many different kinds of exams.

For an examination with very few applicants, you may be told to record your answers in the test booklet itself. Separate answer sheets are much more common. If this separate answer sheet is to be scored by machine – and this is often the case – it is highly important that you mark your answers correctly in order to get credit.

VI. BEFORE THE TEST

YOUR PHYSICAL CONDITION IS IMPORTANT

If you are not well, you can't do your best work on tests. If you are half asleep, you can't do your best either. Here are some tips:

1) Get about the same amount of sleep you usually get. Don't stay up all night before the test, either partying or worrying—DON'T DO IT!
2) If you wear glasses, be sure to wear them when you go to take the test. This goes for hearing aids, too.
3) If you have any physical problems that may keep you from doing your best, be sure to tell the person giving the test. If you are sick or in poor health, you relay cannot do your best on any test. You can always come back and take the test some other time.

Common sense will help you find procedures to follow to get ready for an examination. Too many of us, however, overlook these sensible measures. Indeed, nervousness and fatigue have been found to be the most serious reasons why applicants fail to do their best on civil service tests. Here is a list of reminders:

- Begin your preparation early – Don't wait until the last minute to go scurrying around for books and materials or to find out what the position is all about.
- Prepare continuously – An hour a night for a week is better than an all-night cram session. This has been definitely established. What is more, a night a week for a month will return better dividends than crowding your study into a shorter period of time.
- Locate the place of the exam – You have been sent a notice telling you when and where to report for the examination. If the location is in a different town or otherwise unfamiliar to you, it would be well to inquire the best route and learn something about the building.
- Relax the night before the test – Allow your mind to rest. Do not study at all that night. Plan some mild recreation or diversion; then go to bed early and get a good night's sleep.
- Get up early enough to make a leisurely trip to the place for the test – This way unforeseen events, traffic snarls, unfamiliar buildings, etc. will not upset you.
- Dress comfortably – A written test is not a fashion show. You will be known by number and not by name, so wear something comfortable.
- Leave excess paraphernalia at home – Shopping bags and odd bundles will get in your way. You need bring only the items mentioned in the official notice you received; usually everything you need is provided. Do not bring reference books to the exam. They will only confuse those last minutes and be taken away from you when in the test room.

- Arrive somewhat ahead of time – If because of transportation schedules you must get there very early, bring a newspaper or magazine to take your mind off yourself while waiting.
- Locate the examination room – When you have found the proper room, you will be directed to the seat or part of the room where you will sit. Sometimes you are given a sheet of instructions to read while you are waiting. Do not fill out any forms until you are told to do so; just read them and be prepared.
- Relax and prepare to listen to the instructions
- If you have any physical problem that may keep you from doing your best, be sure to tell the test administrator. If you are sick or in poor health, you really cannot do your best on the exam. You can come back and take the test some other time.

VII. AT THE TEST

The day of the test is here and you have the test booklet in your hand. The temptation to get going is very strong. Caution! There is more to success than knowing the right answers. You must know how to identify your papers and understand variations in the type of short-answer question used in this particular examination. Follow these suggestions for maximum results from your efforts:

1) Cooperate with the monitor

The test administrator has a duty to create a situation in which you can be as much at ease as possible. He will give instructions, tell you when to begin, check to see that you are marking your answer sheet correctly, and so on. He is not there to guard you, although he will see that your competitors do not take unfair advantage. He wants to help you do your best.

2) Listen to all instructions

Don't jump the gun! Wait until you understand all directions. In most civil service tests you get more time than you need to answer the questions. So don't be in a hurry. Read each word of instructions until you clearly understand the meaning. Study the examples, listen to all announcements and follow directions. Ask questions if you do not understand what to do.

3) Identify your papers

Civil service exams are usually identified by number only. You will be assigned a number; you must not put your name on your test papers. Be sure to copy your number correctly. Since more than one exam may be given, copy your exact examination title.

4) Plan your time

Unless you are told that a test is a "speed" or "rate of work" test, speed itself is usually not important. Time enough to answer all the questions will be provided, but this does not mean that you have all day. An overall time limit has been set. Divide the total time (in minutes) by the number of questions to determine the approximate time you have for each question.

5) Do not linger over difficult questions

If you come across a difficult question, mark it with a paper clip (useful to have along) and come back to it when you have been through the booklet. One caution if you do this – be sure to skip a number on your answer sheet as well. Check often to be sure that you have not lost your place and that you are marking in the row numbered the same as the question you are answering.

6) Read the questions

Be sure you know what the question asks! Many capable people are unsuccessful because they failed to read the questions correctly.

7) Answer all questions

Unless you have been instructed that a penalty will be deducted for incorrect answers, it is better to guess than to omit a question.

8) Speed tests

It is often better NOT to guess on speed tests. It has been found that on timed tests people are tempted to spend the last few seconds before time is called in marking answers at random – without even reading them – in the hope of picking up a few extra points. To discourage this practice, the instructions may warn you that your score will be "corrected" for guessing. That is, a penalty will be applied. The incorrect answers will be deducted from the correct ones, or some other penalty formula will be used.

9) Review your answers

If you finish before time is called, go back to the questions you guessed or omitted to give them further thought. Review other answers if you have time.

10) Return your test materials

If you are ready to leave before others have finished or time is called, take ALL your materials to the monitor and leave quietly. Never take any test material with you. The monitor can discover whose papers are not complete, and taking a test booklet may be grounds for disqualification.

VIII. EXAMINATION TECHNIQUES

1) Read the general instructions carefully. These are usually printed on the first page of the exam booklet. As a rule, these instructions refer to the timing of the examination; the fact that you should not start work until the signal and must stop work at a signal, etc. If there are any special instructions, such as a choice of questions to be answered, make sure that you note this instruction carefully.

2) When you are ready to start work on the examination, that is as soon as the signal has been given, read the instructions to each question booklet, underline any key words or phrases, such as least, best, outline, describe and the like. In this way you will tend to answer as requested rather than discover on reviewing your paper that you listed without describing, that you selected the worst choice rather than the best choice, etc.

3) If the examination is of the objective or multiple-choice type – that is, each question will also give a series of possible answers: A, B, C or D, and you are called upon to select the best answer and write the letter next to that answer on your answer paper – it is advisable to start answering each question in turn. There may be anywhere from 50 to 100 such questions in the three or four hours allotted and you can see how much time would be taken if you read through all the questions before beginning to answer any. Furthermore, if you

come across a question or group of questions which you know would be difficult to answer, it would undoubtedly affect your handling of all the other questions.

4) If the examination is of the essay type and contains but a few questions, it is a moot point as to whether you should read all the questions before starting to answer any one. Of course, if you are given a choice – say five out of seven and the like – then it is essential to read all the questions so you can eliminate the two that are most difficult. If, however, you are asked to answer all the questions, there may be danger in trying to answer the easiest one first because you may find that you will spend too much time on it. The best technique is to answer the first question, then proceed to the second, etc.

5) Time your answers. Before the exam begins, write down the time it started, then add the time allowed for the examination and write down the time it must be completed, then divide the time available somewhat as follows:
    - If 3-1/2 hours are allowed, that would be 210 minutes. If you have 80 objective-type questions, that would be an average of 2-1/2 minutes per question. Allow yourself no more than 2 minutes per question, or a total of 160 minutes, which will permit about 50 minutes to review.
    - If for the time allotment of 210 minutes there are 7 essay questions to answer, that would average about 30 minutes a question. Give yourself only 25 minutes per question so that you have about 35 minutes to review.

6) The most important instruction is to read each question and make sure you know what is wanted. The second most important instruction is to time yourself properly so that you answer every question. The third most important instruction is to answer every question. Guess if you have to but include something for each question. Remember that you will receive no credit for a blank and will probably receive some credit if you write something in answer to an essay question. If you guess a letter – say "B" for a multiple-choice question – you may have guessed right. If you leave a blank as an answer to a multiple-choice question, the examiners may respect your feelings but it will not add a point to your score. Some exams may penalize you for wrong answers, so in such cases only, you may not want to guess unless you have some basis for your answer.

7) Suggestions
    a. Objective-type questions
        1. Examine the question booklet for proper sequence of pages and questions
        2. Read all instructions carefully
        3. Skip any question which seems too difficult; return to it after all other questions have been answered
        4. Apportion your time properly; do not spend too much time on any single question or group of questions
        5. Note and underline key words – all, most, fewest, least, best, worst, same, opposite, etc.
        6. Pay particular attention to negatives
        7. Note unusual option, e.g., unduly long, short, complex, different or similar in content to the body of the question
        8. Observe the use of "hedging" words – probably, may, most likely, etc.

9. Make sure that your answer is put next to the same number as the question
10. Do not second-guess unless you have good reason to believe the second answer is definitely more correct
11. Cross out original answer if you decide another answer is more accurate; do not erase until you are ready to hand your paper in
12. Answer all questions; guess unless instructed otherwise
13. Leave time for review

b. Essay questions
1. Read each question carefully
2. Determine exactly what is wanted. Underline key words or phrases.
3. Decide on outline or paragraph answer
4. Include many different points and elements unless asked to develop any one or two points or elements
5. Show impartiality by giving pros and cons unless directed to select one side only
6. Make and write down any assumptions you find necessary to answer the questions
7. Watch your English, grammar, punctuation and choice of words
8. Time your answers; don't crowd material

8) Answering the essay question

Most essay questions can be answered by framing the specific response around several key words or ideas. Here are a few such key words or ideas:

M's: manpower, materials, methods, money, management
P's: purpose, program, policy, plan, procedure, practice, problems, pitfalls, personnel, public relations

a. Six basic steps in handling problems:
1. Preliminary plan and background development
2. Collect information, data and facts
3. Analyze and interpret information, data and facts
4. Analyze and develop solutions as well as make recommendations
5. Prepare report and sell recommendations
6. Install recommendations and follow up effectiveness

b. Pitfalls to avoid
1. Taking things for granted – A statement of the situation does not necessarily imply that each of the elements is necessarily true; for example, a complaint may be invalid and biased so that all that can be taken for granted is that a complaint has been registered
2. Considering only one side of a situation – Wherever possible, indicate several alternatives and then point out the reasons you selected the best one
3. Failing to indicate follow up – Whenever your answer indicates action on your part, make certain that you will take proper follow-up action to see how successful your recommendations, procedures or actions turn out to be
4. Taking too long in answering any single question – Remember to time your answers properly

EXAMINATION SECTION

EXAMINATION SECTION
TEST 1

DIRECTIONS: Each question or incomplete statement is followed by several suggested answers or completions. Select the one that BEST answers the question or completes the statement. *PRINT THE LETTER OF THE CORRECT ANSWER IN THE SPACE AT THE RIGHT.*

1. One of the basic characteristics of a good police supervisor is the courage to accept his supervisory responsibilities and to avoid making excuses and explanations. Of the following, the MOST valid deduction to make from this statement is that the supervisor should

    A. hold subordinates strictly to account so that he is not unjustly blamed
    B. not be required to assume responsibility for the error of a subordinate
    C. not seek to evade blame by referring to the inadequacies of his subordinates
    D. not accept excuses or explanations from his subordinates if they do not perform their duties properly

1.____

2. A rather complex change is to be made in patrol procedures. As a supervising officer, it is your responsibility to make sure that your subordinates are informed of this change. The one of the following courses of action which is MOST likely to result in good performance is for you to

    A. assign one of your best officers to explain the order
    B. distribute an exact copy of the new order as soon as it becomes available
    C. explain the new procedure after your subordinates have had some experience with it
    D. explain the new procedure carefully before it is adopted

2.____

3. As a supervising police officer, you have noticed that, upon the issuance of verbal orders by you to officers, there are seldom any questions asked by them seeking clarification of such orders. You have also noticed that, upon questioning the officers while on patrol, few of them have really understood your orders.
Of the following courses of action, the one which constitutes the BEST solution to this problem is for you to

    A. question the officers immediately following the issuance of your orders
    B. take disciplinary action against those who are not able to understand your orders
    C. issue your orders in written form so that they may be understood more readily
    D. request that your commanding officer issue the orders

3.____

4. A certain officer has a habit of issuing orders and giving directions to other officers on his own responsibility without having received the permission of the supervising officer to do so. Sometimes this occurs in the presence of the supervising officer whose silence on these occasions is interpreted as approval.
This practice is

    A. *bad;* it must result in poorer performance by the other officers
    B. *good;* it helps develop leadership qualities in particular officers who indicate a willingness to accept responsibility

4.____

C. *bad;* it creates an uncertainty in the minds of the other officers about whether a particular order should be obeyed
D. *good;* it makes the work of the supervising officer easier

5. As a supervising police officer, you have observed in your subordinates a consistent lack of attention to several minor patrol duties.
The BEST of the following actions for you to take FIRST is to

   A. attempt to perform these minor duties yourself
   B. take no action on the situation unless this lack of attention spreads to important duties
   C. instruct your subordinates concerning the necessity for performing all duties
   D. request the Chief to speak to your subordinates concerning the situation

6. As a supervising police officer, you have directed a subordinate to follow a specific route while on patrol. You later discover the subordinate patrolling an area outside the designated route.
The one of the following which is the BEST course of action for you to take FIRST is to

   A. explain to the subordinate your reasons for assigning him to the designated route
   B. question the subordinate concerning his reason for not following the designated route
   C. send him back to the designated route immediately
   D. take disciplinary action against the subordinate

7. A newly appointed supervising police officer has decided that he will give equal supervisory attention to each of his subordinates. Such a decision by this supervising officer is

   A. *wise;* all of the subordinates are thereby assured of fair and impartial treatment
   B. *unwise;* the amount of supervisory attention should be varied according to the needs of individual subordinates
   C. *wise;* such a decision will permit the supervising officer to devote more of time to actual patrol
   D. *unwise;* such a decision should be postponed until the Chief can be consulted

8. The one of the following which does NOT constitute an acceptable purpose of the disciplinary process in a police organization is to

   A. improve and maintain the morale of the department
   B. improve the individual whose work falls below defined standards of job performance
   C. provide a strict system of equal punishments for similar offenses
   D. raise or maintain the prestige of the department in the community

9. One of the officers under your supervision has suddenly become very careless in his personal appearance, and his job performance has fallen below the required standard. Questioning of the officer reveals that this condition is due to a serious personal problem.
For you to assist in the solving of this problem is

   A. *improper;* your police background and training make it unlikely that you could provide any real assistance
   B. *proper;* all personal problems of your officers should be your concern

C. *improper;* you would be intruding upon the officer's right to privacy in personal matters
D. *proper;* the officer's personal problem has seriously affected his work

10. A community resident has asked an officer to recommend a good television repairman. For the officer to make such a recommendation would be

    A. *proper;* the officer is performing a service that will help a community resident
    B. *improper;* the officer is not qualified to know a good television repairman from a poor one
    C. *proper;* the officer can thus prevent the community resident from being victimized
    D. *improper;* the officer would be doing something that might affect his effectiveness as a law enforcement officer

11. It is a generally accepted principle of supervision that disciplinary action should be taken quickly when it needs to be taken.
    The one of the following statements which BEST supports the taking of prompt disciplinary action is that

    A. the accuracy of official disciplinary records will thereby be insured
    B. the offender is more likely to feel that the disciplinary action will be severe
    C. the supervisor is more likely to remember the details surrounding the offender's breach of discipline
    D. there is an avoidance of the prolonged aggravation caused by later disposition of the case

12. A supervising police officer has been informed by a certain officer under his supervision that he will soon resign his job and accept employment elsewhere.
    In this situation, the BEST course of action for the supervising officer is to

    A. assign him to the most difficult tasks and tours in order to favor the men remaining
    B. avoid giving him new types of assignments
    C. find out what his new job is and then try to persuade him to remain
    D. refrain from assigning him to work involving any responsibility

13. Officer X has complained to you that Officer Y generally is favored by getting the more desirable assignments. For you, as a supervising police officer, to attempt to explain to Officer X the reason for these assignments of Officer Y would be

    A. *proper;* it is likely to lessen Officer X's objection
    B. *improper;* your authority as a supervisor would be weakened
    C. *proper;* it is needed in order to protect Officer Y from Officer X's resentment and jealousy
    D. *improper;* as a supervisor, there is no need for you to explain the assignments which you make

14. A community resident has complained to the supervising police officer that a certain officer makes a habit of asking him and other residents to buy tickets for dances. An investigation reveals that this is, so.
    Of the following, the BEST course of action for the supervising officer is to

    A. advise the resident that he is under no obligation to buy any such tickets
    B. forbid the officer to sell these tickets, briefly explaining why

C. permit the sale of these tickets only if other groups are allowed equal opportunity to sell tickets to their affairs
D. tell the officer to use discretion in asking people to buy tickets and to avoid asking those who might complain

15. An officer has reprimanded a young boy for playing on the grass in a project. The boy's mother tells the officer that he should be more concerned with arresting criminals than with reprimanding children for petty violations.
Of the following, the BEST answer for the officer to make to this woman is that

   A. children must be taught good conduct by all those concerned for their welfare
   B. damage to public property means higher rents and higher taxes
   C. serious criminals often begin their careers with minor violations
   D. the police force does its best to enforce all laws and regulations

16. In view of the fact that police patrol activity is not able to eliminate all opportunities for criminal behavior, the one of the following procedures which is generally regarded as MOST desirable is for the patrol force to

   A. assign the entire available patrol force to those areas which have the greatest incidence of crime
   B. attempt to give an impression of omnipresence at every hour and in all sections of the community
   C. devote its major efforts to the creation of wholesome influences in a community
   D. keep a substantial patrol force in reserve to answer specific complaints received from the public

17. Although the system of three eight-hour shifts is generally employed by police departments, it would be MORE suitable to provide for overlapping shifts when

   A. an average work load for one shift is substantially less than the other shifts
   B. an hourly work load on one shift fluctuates widely from the average of the shift
   C. the average work load for one shift is substantially greater than the other shifts
   D. the hourly work loads in each of the shifts is almost the same as the average of that shift

18. The highest quality of patrol service results from the permanent assignment of an officer to the same post. The one of the following statements which is the LEAST important advantage of such permanent assignment is that under this system,

   A. it is more likely that events which do not fit into the normal pattern of activity on the post will be noticed
   B. the officer becomes well-acquainted with many persons residing on his post
   C. there is a saving of time and effort due to the familiarity of the officer with his post-relieving point
   D. there is less joint responsibility for conditions on any given post

19. The performance of continuous routine patrol service should generally be provided by the patrol division and not by special divisions.
This statement is

A. *true;* the patrol division should not be subordinated to any other police unit
B. *false;* special divisions frequently are staffed with many of the most competent housing officers
C. *true;* officers engaged in special patrol are less likely to be alert for patrol conditions outside the field of their specialization
D. *false;* special divisions have a basic patrol responsibility equal to that of the patrol division

20. Specialization in the performance of administrative planning duties is not an example of an undesirable specialization of duty being made at the expense of the patrol force. This statement is GENERALLY

    A. *false;* specialization of any kind inevitably results in some depletion of the patrol force
    B. *true;* specialization is desirable to the extent that it efficiently performs part of the actual patrol duty
    C. *false;* this type of duty can be performed efficiently by the individual supervising officer
    D. *true;* these duties cannot be performed by officers in the course of their regular patrol

21. The one of the following which MOST indicates a definite need for the establishment of a specialized enforcement unit, in addition to the regular patrol force, is that

    A. a community group requests that extra enforcement activity be directed towards problems of public morals
    B. a substantial number of patrol personnel have been trained in specialized areas of police work
    C. business interests in the community demand police protection during transfers of cash to banks
    D. the patrol force is unable to perform the total police task in some area

22. The one of the following which indicates the BEST method by which a supervising police officer may check on the quality of patrol performance by the officers under his supervision is to

    A. ask the community residents if they are receiving satisfactory police service
    B. determine the number of arrests for serious crimes made by each officer
    C. observe the officers while they are actually performing patrol
    D. question the more experienced officers concerning the performance of other members of the force

23. The police force should de-emphasize the pursuit of criminals and stress crime prevention.
    For a supervising police officer, this should mean that his CHIEF emphasis should be on the

    A. importance of complete patrol coverage
    B. importance of physical fitness
    C. proficiency of his subordinates with firearms
    D. value of morale in police work

24. Supervising police officers should be instructed how to use manpower to prevent distribution of forces on unproductive assignments.
This statement is

   A. *false;* only time can tell whether any assignment will be unproductive or not
   B. *true;* the supervising officer cannot perform any supervisory duty without such instructions
   C. *false;* assignments should be made solely in response to public demand for police protection
   D. *true;* the assignment of men should be aimed at securing the maximum police protection

25. An officer on patrol is approached by a resident who excitedly informs him that she has just observed a stranger trying the doors of several apartments on the second floor of the project building in which she lives. She also states that the stranger is wearing a dark hat and topcoat. The officer goes to the building and encounters a man hurriedly leaving, who is wearing a gray hat and topcoat. The officer questions him about his presence in the building. The action of the officer was

   A. *poor;* his duty is to go to the second floor as quickly as possible
   B. *good;* everyone in the vicinity of a crime who acts suspiciously should be arrested
   C. *poor;* the tenant stated that the stranger trying the doors was wearing a dark hat and topcoat
   D. *good;* the man about to leave the building may be the same one who was trying the apartment doors

---

KEY (CORRECT ANSWERS)

1. C		11. D	
2. D		12. B	
3. A		13. A	
4. C		14. B	
5. C		15. D	
6. B		16. B	
7. B		17. B	
8. C		18. C	
9. D		19. C	
10. D		20. D	

21. D
22. C
23. A
24. D
25. D

TEST 2

DIRECTIONS: Each question or incomplete statement is followed by several suggested answers or completions. Select the one that BEST answers the question or completes the statement. *PRINT THE LETTER OF THE CORRECT ANSWER IN THE SPACE AT THE RIGHT.*

1. A supervisor who is training several inexperienced subordinates on patrol in the best way to handle the various patrol situations likely to arise should respond with them to calls for their services and

    A. avoid correcting any mistakes as they are made to discuss the overall handling of the situation later
    B. correct all mistakes as they are made and also discuss the overall handling of the situation later
    C. correct all mistakes as they are made and then avoid future discussion of these mistakes
    D. correct serious mistakes as they are made and discuss the overall handling of the situation later

    1.____

2. For an officer who is supervising patrol to make a notation in his memorandum book whenever he strongly reprimands a subordinate verbally is

    A. *inadvisable,* chiefly because an undue amount of supervisory time will be devoted to recording such information
    B. *advisable,* chiefly because the sergeant is developing a fund of information which will be useful in the future handling of the subordinate
    C. *inadvisable,* chiefly because the subordinate may resent such a procedure
    D. *advisable,* chiefly because all subordinates will make greater efforts to improve their job performance since they will not be sure of the nature of the notations

    2.____

3. A supervisor is attempting to discuss some important and practical applications of a new law to police work with a group of his subordinates who have little knowledge of this law. He notices that the group is passive and uninterested in the discussion.
Of the following, it would be BEST for the supervisor to

    A. explain the law and its application carefully and as thoroughly as possible and ask provocative questions
    B. order the group to participate in the discussion since it is for their own good
    C. give the factual information on the law and then stay out of the discussion as much as possible
    D. postpone further discussion until some future time when the group has shown some interest in the law

    3.____

4. While on patrol, a supervisor is required to issue a fairly important order to a subordinate. Due to the pressure of other duties, the supervisor issues the order very quickly and briefly while *on the run.*
An IMPORTANT weakness of the issuance of the order in this manner is that

    A. the subordinate is likely to regard the order as less important than it really is
    B. the supervisor is giving the subordinate more responsibility than is proper
    C. orders require explanation in order to convey the intended meaning
    D. the supervisor is likely to forget this order and to whom it was issued

    4.____

5. In giving orders, a supervisor will give more details at certain times than at other times. The one of the following situations in which the LEAST amount of detail should be given is when the order is concerned with a procedure which

   A. has hazardous features
   B. is of a special or infrequent nature
   C. has been generally performed in a standardized manner
   D. is to be carried out by several subordinates of limited experience

6. Briefing a subordinate on the circumstances which have made an order necessary is desirable MAINLY because the

   A. subordinate thereby has greater respect for the supervisor for his demonstrated knowledge of the job
   B. supervisor is thereby making allowances for differences among subordinates in their ability to understand orders
   C. subordinate will not tend to view the order as a personal or arbitrary command
   D. supervisor will be better able to test the quality of the execution of the order by *follow-up* procedures

7. Disciplinary action will, in most instances, be initiated by the immediate superior of the person to be disciplined. This is so MAINLY because

   A. it permits the higher superiors to be able to devote most of their attention and effort to broader and more generalized problems of administration
   B. it helps to develop a forceful image of the immediate superior which will serve to prevent other overt acts of misconduct by other subordinates
   C. the immediate superior is the one most qualified to make recommendations as to the severity of punishment to be applied
   D. the immediate superior is usually in the best position to observe derelictions of duty requiring some kind of corrective action

8. Having decided to institute disciplinary action against a subordinate in his command, a supervisor speaks to the subordinate for the purpose of informing him of the action to be taken.
   At this interview, it would be LEAST advisable for the supervisor to explain to the subordinate

   A. the procedural steps which will follow the institution of disciplinary action
   B. the specific reason for the disciplinary action
   C. that the purpose of discipline is the punishment of the offender
   D. what is expected of the subordinate in the future, especially as related to the behavior which resulted in disciplinary action being taken

9. The repeated use by a superior officer of a call for volunteers to get a job done is objectionable MAINLY because

   A. it may create a feeling of animosity between the volunteers and the non-volunteers
   B. it may indicate that the superior is avoiding responsibility for making assignments which will be most productive
   C. it is an indication that the superior is not familiar with the individual capabilities of his men
   D. it is unfair to men who, for valid reasons, do not or cannot volunteer

10. Of the following statements concerning subordinates, expressions to a supervisor of their opinions and feelings concerning work situations, the one which is MOST correct is that

    A. by listening and responding to such expressions the supervisor encourages the development of complaints
    B. the lack of such expressions should indicate to the supervisor that there is a high level of job satisfaction
    C. the more the supervisor listens to and responds to such expressions, the more he demonstrates lack of supervisory ability
    D. by listening and responding to such expressions, the supervisor will enable many subordinates to understand and solve their own problems on the job

11. Usually one thinks of communication as a single step, essentially that of transmitting an idea. Actually, however, this is only part of a total process, the FIRST step of which should be

    A. the prompt dissemination of the idea to those who may be affected by it
    B. motivating those affected to take the required action
    C. clarifying the idea in one's own mind
    D. deciding to whom the idea is to be communicated

12. Research studies on patterns of informal communication have concluded that most individuals in a group tend to be passive recipients of news, while a few make it their business to spread it around in an organization.
    With this conclusion in mind, it would be MOST correct for the supervisor to attempt to identify these few individuals and

    A. give them the complete facts on important matters in advance of others
    B. inform the other subordinates of the identity of these few individuals so that their influence may be minimized
    C. keep them straight on the facts on important matters
    D. warn them to cease passing along any information to others

13. The one of the following which is the PRINCIPAL advantage of making an oral report is that it

    A. affords an immediate opportunity for two-way communication between the subordinate and superior
    B. is an easy method for the superior to use in transmitting information to others of equal rank
    C. saves the time of all concerned
    D. permits more precise pinpointing of praise or blame by means of follow-up questions by the superior

14. Supervisory training is designed to develop skills in human relationships while work-skill training attempts to alter the relationship between a person and a machine or material of some sort.
    The one of the following which MOST accurately describes an important difference between these two types of training is that

A. resistance to work-skill training is likely to be greater than resistance to supervisory training
B. skills acquired from supervisory training should be less flexible than skills acquired from work-skill training
C. skills acquired from supervisory training are usually less directly and routinely applied than skills acquired from work-skill training
D. trainees are more apt to feel more secure in attempting to utilize skills acquired through supervisory training than those acquired from work-skill training

15. The quantity and quality of work performed by one subordinate is below the level that he is capable of attaining. Because of this, the supervisor gives this subordinate the least difficult assignments only.
This action taken by the supervisor is

   A. *poor,* chiefly because the subordinate should be motivated to perform work of greater responsibility
   B. *good,* chiefly because each subordinate should be allowed to work in the manner he finds most satisfactory
   C. *poor,* chiefly because the supervisor should make his assignments such that all subordinates are given an equal amount of work and responsibility
   D. *good,* chiefly because otherwise the supervisor will have to give a greater amount of supervisory attention to this subordinate than to other subordinates

16. It has been the practice in some communities to substantially base the efficiency rating of police commanders on incidence of crime.
This practice is inadvisable MAINLY because

   A. crime figures also reflect many community factors beyond the control of the commander
   B. such figures may be incomplete and unreliable
   C. there is little or no relation between such figures and police efficiency
   D. there is a great need for improved techniques of processing and analysis of crime figures

17. Even though officers are assigned on a permanent basis to tours of duty at night, experts in plant security recommend that arrangements be made for them to make a complete tour of the premises during the daytime.
The CHIEF reason for this suggestion is to

   A. enable them to coordinate their patrol work better with that of the officers assigned to daytime duty
   B. discover those areas in which teenage groups congregate during the day and which are, therefore, most vulnerable to night-time crime
   C. allow them to become more familiar with the general layout of the premises and with specific locations that may be of importance to them in their work
   D. give them a clearer daytime view of the exact conditions they may expect to encounter during their tours of duty at night

18. It has been suggested that housing officers on duty at night record the names of all Authority employees remaining in or leaving the project considerably after their normal working hours.
The CHIEF reason for taking this precaution would be to

A. assist the housing police force in interrogating the supervisors of these employees to determine whether they have any valid reason for remaining after their working hours
B. enable the housing police force to determine more promptly whether these employees are involved in any illegal activity during their off-duty hours
C. assist the housing police force to direct its questioning to these employees if it later develops that something improper occurred during this period of time
D. enable the housing police force to scrutinize more closely the activities of these employees during their regular working hours

19. The one of the following which is a distinct advantage of an organization's special police force over the regular police force is that the special police force GENERALLY

    A. has a limited area of jurisdiction in which only certain types of crimes occur
    B. has a limited responsibility for exercising diligence in patrol
    C. is able to limit its surveillance to only those persons who are not tenants or employees
    D. knows that most persons with whom it comes in contact on post are known to it as tenants or employees of the organization

20. From a management point of view, the BEST of the following reasons why it is better for police to emphasize the prevention of theft and vandalism, rather than the detection of such crimes or the apprehension of persons involved, is that preventive measures generally

    A. expedite the more prompt reporting of acts of vandalism and thefts because any actual occurrence of such offenses would be made more obvious
    B. minimize the need for the more unpleasant and costly procedures involved in apprehending and prosecuting guilty employees
    C. result in offenders being easily caught in the act of committing the crime
    D. involve stricter screening of employees and thus prevent any would-be criminals from becoming employees

21. It is generally recommended that the security division or special force of an organization be organized and trained in the measures needed to disperse or control a milling crowd and prevent it from turning into a rioting mob CHIEFLY in order to

    A. avoid the necessity of seeking outside assistance in quelling a purely local disturbance involving the organization
    B. quickly isolate and apprehend the leaders of the mob so that the police can take proper punitive action
    C. prevent injury or death to persons and damage to organization plant and equipment
    D. prevent the mob from spreading out into territory where the special police force has no jurisdiction

22. The CHIEF reason why the issuance of identification badges should be carefully controlled and why one should never be reissued with the same serial number as one which has been previously reported lost is to

A. insure against duplications of identification and establish a clear record of who is authorized to possess a particular badge
B. minimize the possibility of their being stolen or counterfeited by unauthorized persons
C. make sure that identification badges are returned
D. prevent unauthorized persons from mutilating or altering a validly issued identification badge

23. The rotation of officers has been recommended, in terms of both time and place of operation.
    The CHIEF of the following reasons for applying this recommendation to experienced officers would be to

    A. enable them to gain more experience by exposing them to the different supervisory methods of various superior officers
    B. keep them alert by making them uncertain as to the varying degrees of diligence required by the different superior officers to whom they are assigned
    C. prevent them from becoming overly friendly with the residents and shopkeepers in the neighborhood
    D. make them more aware of problems existing in the various communities

24. Supervisors often feel that police recruits today do not accept direction as willingly as in the past.
    The one of the following which is the MOST likely explanation for such a reaction by some recruits is the

    A. emphasis on individuality found in the home and in the school which tends to substitute tolerance and freedom for strict discipline
    B. increasingly complex nature of society which does not permit authoritarian concepts of discipline
    C. negative reaction to authority of men who have fulfilled a required military service obligation
    D. current notion that frequent direction by superiors constitutes undemocratic supervision

25. Police officers on patrol are constantly warned to be on the alert for suspicious persons, actions, and circumstances. With this in mind, a supervisor should emphasize the need for them to

    A. be cautious and suspicious when dealing officially with any civilian, regardless of the latter's overt actions or the circumstances surrounding his dealings with the police
    B. become thoroughly familiar with the usual on their posts so as to be better able to detect the unusual
    C. take aggressive police action immediately against any unusual person or condition detected on their posts, regardless of any other circumstances
    D. keep looking for the unusual persons, actions, and circumstances on their posts and pay less attention to the usual occurrences

KEY (CORRECT ANSWERS)

1. D
2. B
3. A
4. A
5. C

6. C
7. D
8. C
9. B
10. D

11. C
12. C
13. A
14. C
15. A

16. A
17. C
18. C
19. D
20. B

21. C
22. A
23. C
24. A
25. B

TEST 3

DIRECTIONS: Each question or incomplete statement is followed by several suggested answers or completions. Select the one that BEST answers the question or completes the statement. *PRINT THE LETTER OF THE CORRECT ANSWER IN THE SPACE AT THE RIGHT.*

1. The most competent leaders seldom have to resort to a display of authority. Of the following, the MOST important quality of this type of leader is that he

    A. is able to inspire subordinates to perform satisfactorily
    B. makes sure that his men know the point beyond which punitive action will be taken
    C. secures compliance with orders by formalized disciplinary procedures
    D. secures compliance with orders by implied threats of disciplinary action

2. Demands for more police officers are frequently made by police administrators before they have first adopted methods that will assure a more effective use of the present forces.
   In view of this statement, the BEST of the following guides to the most effective utilization of police personnel is the

    A. analysis of reports, complaints, and statistics to indicate needed services
    B. demands of various community groups for special kinds of police protection
    C. fullest use of new scientific equipment in records management
    D. requests of commanders of specialized units who seek to increase the effectiveness of their units by the assignment of additional men

3. An organization such as a police agency is not generally confronted by such unique problems as to make impossible the application of certain administrative principles that have been found applicable in other organizations.
   Of the following, the MOST valid deduction to make from this statement is that

    A. practices of other organizations reveal that police problems are not generally susceptible to solution by standardized management techniques
    B. questions of size are relevant in evaluating the applicability of common administrative principles
    C. some management guides can serve both police and non-police administrators equally well
    D. superficial familiarity with police organizations often leads to the application of invalid administrative techniques

4. Formal police training programs should generally be conducted during the officers' off-duty time; otherwise, the public funds allotted to police services are not being properly used.
   This statement is GENERALLY

    A. *false;* close supervision during the actual performance of duties provides the only practical training technique
    B. *true;* the most effective training is usually conducted in an environment completely different from the one in which job performance takes place
    C. *true;* only those training activities which relate to the performance of extremely difficult duties should be conducted during on-duty time
    D. *false;* more effective performance of duties by the trainees will compensate for any on-duty time devoted to training

5. The ultimate responsibility for police training lies with the top echelon of command, and the supervising police officer should not properly be held accountable for any part of this supervisory function.
   This statement is

   A. *true;* the supervising police officer should devote the major portion of his time to the performance of patrol
   B. *false;* the supervising police officer is in a key position to assist in training
   C. *true;* the duty of a supervising police officer to correct the improper patrol performance of subordinates cannot be classified as training
   D. *false;* the supervising police officer's primary responsibility is the training of subordinates

6. Periodic training of all police personnel, experienced officers as well as recruits, is a necessary requirement for effective police operations.
   This statement is GENERALLY

   A. *false;* methods of police operation are relatively stable and, therefore, additional training is unnecessary
   B. *true;* experienced personnel and recruits both require continued training at essentially the same level
   C. *false;* such training would undermine the morale of the experienced officers and seriously affect their job performance
   D. *true;* the original training may be forgotten or made obsolete by changing community conditions and improved methods

7. There is considerable merit to the idea that the police agency have only one telephone number listed in the telephone directory so that the general public, when seeking police assistance, will be required to contact a central complaint desk.
   The one of the following which is the MOST important advantage of this procedure is that

   A. direct public contact with the central complaint desk will insure that the most appropriate police action will be taken
   B. it makes less likely the possibility of a complaint being ignored or not investigated
   C. it makes unnecessary any future public contact with the local police unit
   D. it prevents any complaints from being registered in any local police unit

8. A system of complete decentralization of police records, with the line operating units maintaining their own records, constitutes the most advisable system.
   This statement is GENERALLY

   A. *false;* decentralization of record keeping tends to turn the line operating units into small and almost independent police organizations
   B. *true;* decentralization of record keeping fixes responsibility in a manner superior to the centralization of record keeping
   C. *false;* such complete decentralization of records would prevent any coordination of the line operating units
   D. *true;* police records should remain in the unit of their origin so that ready reference may be made to them

9. Much of the difficulty encountered in the process of administrative communication arises from a failure to realize that many words have varied, rather than a single, meaning. Accordingly, in issuing complex orders, it would be MOST important for the newly appointed supervising police officer to

   A. carefully check the meaning of difficult words in proposed orders
   B. issue written orders, rather than verbal orders, wherever possible
   C. review and discuss the orders with his subordinates
   D. revise the wording of all orders in order to clarify their meaning

10. As a supervising police officer, you have informed your subordinates that the Chief wants them to come to him directly at any suitable time to discuss problems, grievances, or suggestions for improvement of patrol performance. You have noticed, after a lapse of several months, that none of your subordinates have gone to the Chief for any of these purposes.
    The one of the following which is the LEAST likely explanation of this reluctance on the part of your subordinates is

    A. the natural reluctance of subordinates to freely express their ideas in the presence of higher authority
    B. that the subordinates may be reluctant to bypass your authority as their immediate supervisor
    C. the fear of being considered *troublemakers* by other superior officers in the department
    D. that good supervision has completely eliminated problems, grievances, and the need for suggestions

11. As a supervising police officer, you feel that a certain officer under your supervision is responsible for starting several unfounded rumors concerning police matters in the precinct.
    Of the following possible courses of action, the one which would be the MOST effective in dealing with the problem is to

    A. ignore the situation since none of the rumors contained any elements of truth
    B. provide sufficient facts about police matters in the precinct to establish a basis upon which rumors may be evaluated
    C. institute formal disciplinary action against the suspected officer
    D. speak to your subordinates, as a group, on the undesirable effects of spreading false information

12. Although the increasing complexity of police work strongly favors the specialist, experienced administrators are alert to the dangers in this tendency and strive to maintain flexible arrangements whenever specialized techniques threaten unity of action.
    Of the following, the MOST valid conclusion from this statement is that

    A. complexity of police work requires specialization to insure unity of action
    B. flexibility is needed to offset the occasional undesirable effects of specialization
    C. the role of the specialist in police work has become more important due to the influence of experienced administrators
    D. unity of action, although increased by specialization, can at the same time be inflexible because of police complexity

13. The quality of police service is more strongly influenced by the competence of the individual members of the force than by any other single factor.
The one of the following aspects of police administration which contributes LEAST to the development of such competence is the

    A. absence of morale-destroying influences
    B. promptness and certainty of disciplinary procedures
    C. existence of a suitable recruit training program
    D. survey of needed changes in organizational structure

14. Some law enforcement agencies do not wait for the legal disposition of an arrest case by the courts but close the arrest record when their custody of a prisoner ends. Such a procedure is GENERALLY considered to be

    A. *good;* strict impartiality by the police in the administration of criminal law requires that they be unaffected by either the conviction or acquittal of a prisoner
    B. *good;* the long delays frequently accompanying court procedure would unduly add to the work involved in the record keeping function
    C. *poor;* the legal disposition of a case should have some bearing on evaluating the work of the agency
    D. *poor;* court dispositions provide the only sure indication of the quality of the police investigative procedures

15. A maintenance man continually brings to the attention of a housing officer matters of a minor nature about building upkeep which are not the proper concern of the housing officer force. The housing officer has told the maintenance man that these problems are not a concern of the housing police personnel. However, the maintenance man continues to bring these matters to the attention of the housing officer. The housing officer tells his supervising officer about the situation.
Of the following, the BEST course of action for the supervising officer to take is to

    A. advise the housing officer to listen to the complaints of the maintenance man and then to ignore them
    B. ask the housing manager to take steps to change the conduct of the maintenance man
    C. have the housing officer transferred to another assignment so that he will not come in contact with the maintenance man
    D. suggest to the housing manager that the maintenance man be transferred since the latter is interfering with police duties

16. The one of the following factors which provides the BEST indication of the number of officers to be assigned to the inspection of store doors during the night hours is the

    A. average distance between the stores to be inspected
    B. number of complaints received from the owners of the stores to be inspected
    C. number of man-hours required to perform these inspections properly
    D. number of stores that are to be inspected

17. When properly performed, patrol plays a leading role in the accomplishment of the police purpose of crime prevention CHIEFLY by

    A. apprehending offenders and impressing them with the omnipotence of the police
    B. being the only form of police service that directly attempts to eliminate the opportunities for crime

C. gaining public support by the prompt investigation of offenses and recovery of stolen property
D. influencing public attitudes against crime in its routine daily associations with the public

18. The theory of police patrol which, if properly applied, should have the GREATEST deterrent effect on crime is that which favors patrolling

   A. all areas in such a manner as to make the police officers as unnoticeable as possible
   B. all areas in such a manner as to attract the maximum of attention to the police
   C. areas of high incidence of crime in an obvious manner and on a frequent and fixed schedule
   D. areas of low incidence of crime obviously and irregularly and areas of high incidence of crime on an irregular schedule and attracting a minimum of attention

19. It has been said that police patrol should aim at giving the impression of omnipresence at all times.
The one of the following which is the PRIMARY reason for this statement is that generally the

   A. planning for successful theft must be changed by the potential offender's expectation of apprehension
   B. potential thief's desire to steal is diminished by the presence of a uniformed officer
   C. potential thief's belief in the opportunity for successful theft is diminished by his expectation of apprehension
   D. potential thief's desire to steal is diminished by his expectation of apprehension

20. Whenever new tasks and duties are assigned to the police force, the question arises as to whether they should be assigned to the regular patrol force or to a specialized unit.
It would be MOST desirable in such a situation for the new tasks and duties to be so assigned as to give the

   A. regular patrol force all tasks and duties which it can perform as well as if done by specialists and which do not interfere with regular patrol duties
   B. specialized units all tasks and duties which they can perform as efficiently as the regular patrol force
   C. regular patrol force only those tasks and duties which are clearly in keeping with patrol duties and which are of a non-specialized nature
   D. specialized units all those tasks and duties which are of a specialized nature regardless of their relationship to regular patrol duties

21. An undesirable result of specialization in police work is the

   A. assignment to regular patrol officers of the primary responsibility for the enforcement of regulations in specialized areas of enforcement
   B. assignment of regular patrol officers to render many services to the specialized branches of service
   C. performance by patrol officers during the course of their regular patrol of tasks which can be performed by specialists at any other time
   D. performance by specialists of tasks that should be performed by patrol officers in the course of their regular patrol

22. There has been a marked trend during the past thirty years toward a greater public demand for extra services from the patrol force and also a trend toward increased specialization in police work.
The CHIEF drawback to both of these tendencies is the

    A. difficulty of choosing the members of the force to be assigned to both these tasks
    B. decrease in the number of members of the force available for assignment to patrol
    C. poorer technical knowledge of the patrol sergeant in his supervisory dealings with police specialists
    D. reduction in authority and prestige of the members of the force assigned to patrol duties in contrast to that of those assigned to special units

23. It is not enough for a police agency's services to be of a high quality; attention must also be given to the acceptability of these services to the general public. This statement is GENERALLY

    A. *false;* a superior quality of police service automatically wins public support
    B. *true;* the police cannot generally progress beyond the understanding and support of the public
    C. *false;* the acceptance by the public of police services determines their quality
    D. *true;* the police are generally unable to engage in any effective enforcement activity without public support

24. Final decisions regarding quality and extent of police services to be provided should rest with those politically responsible for the conduct of a city's affairs.
The PRINCIPAL reason for this point of view is that

    A. only those officials responsible for the overall conduct of city affairs have the authority to make such decisions
    B. city and state legislation determine the limits of the activities of the police
    C. these officials have the advantage of readily available technical advice and information from police officials
    D. the level of governmental services is, in the final analysis, dependent solely upon budgetary considerations

25. Of the following, the LEAST likely way in which a records system may serve a supervising police officer is in

    A. developing a sympathetic and cooperative public attitude toward the police
    B. improving the quality of supervision by permitting a check on the accomplishment of subordinates
    C. permitting a precise prediction of the exact crime incidence in specific categories for the following year
    D. helping to take the guesswork out of the distribution of the force

KEY (CORRECT ANSWERS)

1. A
2. A
3. C
4. D
5. B

6. D
7. B
8. A
9. C
10. D

11. B
12. B
13. D
14. C
15. B

16. C
17. B
18. B
19. C
20. A

21. D
22. B
23. B
24. A
25. A

EXAMINATION SECTION
TEST 1

DIRECTIONS: Each question or incomplete statement is followed by several suggested answers or completions. Select the one that BEST answers the question or completes the statement. *PRINT THE LETTER OF THE CORRECT ANSWER IN THE SPACE AT THE RIGHT.*

1. Certain charts showing police accomplishments may properly be placed in locations where they may be reviewed by the public.
   However, it would NOT be appropriate to display publicly a chart showing the

   A. percentage of cases cleared by arrest
   B. number of citations and notices of violation issued per month
   C. percentage of stolen property recovered
   D. records of arrests made by individual officers

2. Of the following, an order given by a superior officer will MOST likely be accepted and carried out without resentment if it is

   A. stated in a simple manner
   B. given as a direct command
   C. framed as a request
   D. given by an immediate superior

3. Written orders are often classified in three categories: general, special, and personnel. The one of the following that would MOST appropriately be considered a general order is an order

   A. creating an agency-wide records system
   B. promoting a group of officers
   C. concerning crowd control at a stadium during the football season
   D. concerning security protection during the visit of a head of state

4. There is a very strong tradition in this country which holds that it is improper for a municipal chief executive to be involved in the internal affairs of a police agency. All of the following have contributed to the development of this tradition EXCEPT

   A. widespread awareness of the history of improper involvement by elected officials
   B. a belief that police responsibility is prescribed and leaves no room for additional guidance and direction
   C. statutory provisions which establish the chief executive's responsibility for overseeing police operations
   D. reluctance of chief executives to become involved in highly technical matters best left to police administrators

5. Organization charts in a police department are normally used for all of the following purposes EXCEPT

   A. identifying functional responsibilities of the various elements
   B. indicating organizational units which require greater specialization
   C. presenting diagrammatically an organization's formal structure
   D. serving as a pictorial representation of personnel distributions

6. In police work, emergencies sometimes arise which require overtime assignments. Typically, some men will be happy to work overtime, while others will object to any change in their regular schedule.
In this situation, the BEST policy for a superior officer to follow in assigning overtime work is to

   A. restrict overtime assignments to those employees who are considered to be doing the best work
   B. assign overtime without regard to individual preference so that all the men work approximately the same amount
   C. establish a schedule whereby each man works overtime when his turn comes up
   D. rotate overtime assignments as much as possible among employees who are willing to work additional hours

7. Assume that you, a newly assigned superior officer, must assign two men to a job that requires close cooperation. You are considering two men who are mutual friends for this assignment.
To place friends together on such an assignment would generally be

   A. *advisable,* chiefly because friends are likely to be more productive than men who are not friends
   B. *inadvisable,* chiefly because this arrangement will lead to more talking on the job and less work
   C. *advisable,* chiefly because subordinates should be allowed to select the persons they will work with
   D. *inadvisable,* chiefly because a precedent will be established which would not apply in other situations

8. Assume that a superior officer is reviewing a report submitted by one of his subordinates upon the completion of an assignment. It appears from the report that the subordinate has not carried out his assignment properly, although the superior officer is not sure what mistake was made.
Of the following, it would be MOST advisable for the superior officer to

   A. try to get all the pertinent facts before speaking to the subordinate
   B. wait until the subordinate discovers the mistake for himself so that he may learn from it
   C. wait until he has a better alternative to offer the subordinate before correcting him
   D. indicate to the subordinate that the report is not satisfactory and let him attempt to work out his own solution

9. In many organizations, including police departments, groups often evolve their own leadership.
In order to work with informal leaders and build up good relations with them, it would be advisable for a superior officer to do all of the following EXCEPT

   A. ask the advice of the informal leader on human relations and other problems
   B. request the informal leader's assistance in getting subordinates to perform tasks that they resent
   C. give certain information to the informal leader first
   D. assign the informal leader to help train other subordinates

10. The number of subordinates an individual can supervise effectively is influenced by several factors. Below are four situations which might affect this number:
    I. Subordinates are well-trained and experienced
    II. The work is complicated and somewhat dangerous
    III. The supervisor is newly assigned and unfamiliar with certain aspects of the work
    IV. The work is centralized and performed in a limited area.

    Which of the following choices lists all of the above situations which would tend to DECREASE the number of subordinates one individual can supervise effectively?

    A. I, III, and IV, but not II
    B. II and III, but not I and IV
    C. I, II, and III, but not IV
    D. I and IV, but not II and III

11. A newly assigned superior officer regularly discusses many matters with his subordinates, including personal matters that are not directly related to the job.
    All of the following may be considered advantages of this superior officer's policy EXCEPT:

    A. The superior officer's task will be easier when he must rely on formal authority to maintain discipline
    B. Good informal relations may improve communication on problems related to work
    C. The superior officer will be better able to understand his subordinates' behavior and how to deal with it
    D. Subordinates have an opportunity to bring up problems that may be bothering them

12. In making work assignments, some police departments attempt to limit the variety of tasks assigned to each officer.
    This practice is generally

    A. *advisable,* mainly because rotation of assignments increases the time spent on coordination
    B. *inadvisable,* mainly because many tasks should be combined into a single function
    C. *advisable,* mainly because individual productivity will increase when officers specialize
    D. *inadvisable,* mainly because lesser efficiency results when officers perform a variety of tasks

13. One approach to motivation is for the supervisor to emphasize his own authority and constantly exert pressure upon his subordinates.
    Of the following, the MOST likely result of this approach is that

    A. employees will work only hard enough to avoid punishment
    B. individuals will attempt to impress the supervisor by surpassing group work standards
    C. production will improve on a long-run basis
    D. departmental standards will be accepted after an initial period of employee resistance

14. As part of the disciplinary process, some organizations publish or post prominently the names of employees who have been disciplined with a concise description of the charges brought against them.
    Of the following, the basic purpose of this procedure is to

    A. prevent rumors and speculation concerning the punitive actions that have been taken
    B. identify those employees whose conduct has fallen below acceptable standards
    C. increase the severity of the punishment by publicizing the names of the chastised employees
    D. indicate to all employees the types of acts the organization will not tolerate

15. In terms of accomplishing organizational objectives, the main purposes of discipline include all of the following EXCEPT

    A. obtaining compliance with established rules of conduct
    B. punishing those who fail to conform with accepted standards
    C. developing self-control and character among subordinates
    D. fostering orderliness and operational efficiency

16. A superior officer who wishes to instruct subordinates in new procedures or methods should be familiar with the following steps in the teaching process:
    I. Present information or skills in an orderly and systematic manner
    II. Measure the learner's understanding and evaluate progress
    III. Focus the learner's attention and stimulate interest
    IV. Provide an opportunity for the learner to apply what he has learned

    Which of the following choices lists these steps in the order in which they should be taken in the training process?

    A. III, II, I, IV
    B. II, I, III, IV
    C. III, I, IV, II
    D. I, III, II, IV

17. In many large organizations, a grapevine supplements the formal communications system.
    In a police department, the existence of a grapevine should GENERALLY be considered

    A. *undesirable,* chiefly because rumors are almost always false and exaggerated and interfere with efficient operation
    B. *desirable,* chiefly because it stimulates employee interest in the department's objectives
    C. *undesirable,* chiefly because it tends to undermine the effectiveness of official communications
    D. *desirable,* chiefly because it often provides a personal and flexible method of transmitting information quickly

18. Following are four factors which might contribute to riots:
    I. Fears often develop from imaginary causes and influence the actions of individuals and entire communities
    II. An individual who feels himself outside the mainstream of life will often identify with extremism and oppose society
    III. For an outburst to occur, it is necessary that a considerable part of the community feel repressed
    IV. A group's sense of security may be jeopardized when they are forced to accept large numbers of outsiders

    Which of the following choices lists ALL of the above factors which do contribute to riots?

    A. I and IV, but not II and III
    B. II and IV, but not I and III
    C. I, III, and IV, but not II
    D. I, II, III, and IV

18.____

19. Assume that a superior officer wishes to establish a work schedule that assigns men to various types of duty on a rotating and systematic basis.
    The one of the following which would be LEAST likely to result from such scheduling is the

    A. elimination of technical work for which specialists are required
    B. development by subordinates of the overall skills and abilities necessary in law enforcement
    C. improvement of motivation and morale resulting from greater interest provided by the variety of work
    D. awareness among subordinates of the superior officer's fairness and impartiality in the assignment of work

19.____

20. All organizations need a system of quality control to insure that administrative policies are being followed with precision and uniformity.
    In a large and decentralized police department, this control can MOST effectively be accomplished by

    A. an internal investigation unit
    B. line supervisors
    C. a staff inspection unit
    D. report-review

20.____

21. Superior officers may choose to give orders in various ways depending on circumstances and the subordinates involved.
    It would be MOST advisable for a supervisor to give an implied or indirect order when

    A. he is dealing with relatively inexperienced subordinates
    B. he wishes to develop a subordinate's initiative
    C. it is necessary to follow up and closely supervise the subordinate's performance
    D. the subordinate has been indifferent to standard operating rules

21.____

22. The nature of organization structure in a police department does not permit a perfectly uniform relationship of a supervisor's rank to the size of subdivisions or the complexity of the job.
All of the following are consistent with the concept of a balanced organization structure EXCEPT

    A. giving higher rank to difficult and complex positions even though supervisory responsibilities are minimal
    B. utilizing lower ranks for higher-level responsibilities
    C. providing equal rank for subordinates supervised directly by the same supervisor
    D. basing the structure on the maximum number of supervisory levels necessary for control

23. One method that has been suggested to improve the quality of law enforcement is coordination and consolidation of police services among various agencies.
The one of the following areas in which consolidation of police services would be LEAST appropriate is

    A. criminal investigation   B. communications
    C. laboratory services   D. training

24. In most police departments, decisions governing the force's patrol methods are based principally upon

    A. analysis of crime trends
    B. tradition
    C. availability of personnel
    D. public relations considerations

25. A superior officer must learn to recognize and deal with the problem of frustration among some of his subordinates. The one of the following methods of dealing with frustration that is LEAST likely to be successful is

    A. keeping channels of communication open in order to be aware of employee attitudes
    B. allowing subordinates to gain insight into their problems by discussing them with the supervisor
    C. encouraging subordinates to select goals which require hard work to achieve so that their efforts will be directed toward constructive activity
    D. changing certain assignments in order to provide more favorable working conditions

KEY (CORRECT ANSWERS)

1. D
2. C
3. A
4. C
5. B

6. D
7. A
8. A
9. B
10. B

11. A
12. C
13. A
14. D
15. B

16. C
17. D
18. D
19. A
20. C

21. B
22. D
23. A
24. B
25. C

TEST 2

DIRECTIONS: Each question or incomplete statement is followed by several suggested answers or completions. Select the one that BEST answers the question or completes the statement. *PRINT THE LETTER OF THE CORRECT ANSWER IN THE SPACE AT THE RIGHT.*

1. In order to establish good relationships with his subordinates, a superior officer attempts to behave the same way toward all of his men.
   This superior officer's approach is generally

   A. *desirable;* this policy will avoid charges of favoritism
   B. *undesirable;* he should try to adjust his behavior to his subordinates' individual needs
   C. *desirable;* his subordinates will respect the superior officer's efforts to show his concern for them
   D. *undesirable;* his attempt to show interest may be seen as meddling

2. Subordinates will obey an order more willingly when they respect the legitimacy of the order. What individuals perceive as legitimate depends largely on the views of their associates.
   It can be deduced from this statement that the one of the following ways in which subordinates are MOST likely to cooperate with a superior officer is by

   A. working harder whenever the superior officer requests increased productivity
   B. agreeing to accept unpleasant working conditions which the superior officer is unable to correct
   C. accepting assignments that are outside the limits of their customary duties
   D. taking informal disciplinary action against those who violate group expectations by not obeying legitimate orders

3. The one of the following which should NOT be considered a primary objective of a complaint investigation policy is protection of the

   A. integrity and reputation of the force
   B. department from the actions of review boards
   C. public interest
   D. accused employee from the consequences of unjust accusation

4. Some large police departments have attempted to apply advances in technology to law enforcement. Technological contributions are expected in all of the following areas EXCEPT

   A. dispatching personnel more quickly to calls which are most likely to escalate into grave disorders
   B. altering police deployment in response to changing community crime patterns
   C. assisting the police in identifying persons and determining whether they are currently wanted by the police
   D. increasing police-radio frequency usage and decreasing the use of teletype networks

5. Men who possess power might have to learn to behave as if they had none if they wish to increase the tendency among their subordinates to solve problems by constructive thinking.
According to this statement, the one of the following which would be MOST advisable for a superior officer interested in improving the performance of his subordinates is to

   A. direct the efforts of subordinates into areas which will achieve organizational objectives
   B. increase the amount of information which is provided to subordinates
   C. view his role in terms of helping his subordinates rather than telling them what to do
   D. indicate which actions are most appropriate whenever difficult problems arise

6. In police report writing, it is important to distinguish between statements of observed facts and conclusions derived from facts.
Which of the following sentences could BEST be described as expressing a conclusion rather than a statement of fact?

   A. The defendant made a threatening gesture toward the victim.
   B. Wilson refused to speak to the Lieutenant and asked several times to see a lawyer.
   C. When arrested, the defendant was carrying the victim's cigarette case.
   D. Jones heard the defendant say that he had been drinking shortly before the accident.

7. Police administration involves several interrelated processes whose objective is the achievement of organizational goals.
The one of the following administrative processes which should generally precede the others is

   A. organizing   B. directing
   C. planning   D. controlling

8. Following are four statements which might reflect a superior officer's attitudes and beliefs concerning himself and his subordinates:
   I. A worker who learns slowly does not remember better than one who learns rapidly
   II. Supervisors form most of their opinions by logical reasoning
   III. Supervisors can generally size up a worker very accurately in an interview
   IV. A worker who sets high goals for himself is likely to accomplish more and be happier

Which of the following choices lists ALL of the above statements with which psychologists are in general agreement?

   A. I, II, and III, but not IV
   B. II, III, and IV, but not I
   C. I and II, but not III and IV
   D. I, but not II, III, and IV

9. It has been stated that daily reports should be based on calendar days, from midnight to midnight, rather than 24-hour periods established by shift changes, such as 7:00 A.M. to 7:00 A.M.
The PRINCIPAL advantage of basing daily reports on calendar days is that

A. reports will be comparable with those prepared in cooperation with other agencies
B. the amount of outside assistance required to complete the report is reduced
C. changes in shift reporting times will not destroy the comparative value of the reports
D. the interpretation and prediction of needs for police services are significantly improved

10. According to the principles of organization, a police force should be organized into units primarily on the basis of

    A. the nature of the tasks to be performed
    B. the level of authority needed to accomplish objectives
    C. clearly defined lines of control
    D. the amount of supervision required at the level of execution

11. To be effective in dealing with human relations problems, a police officer should understand the nature of prejudice.
    Of the following, it would be INCORRECT to state that prejudiced persons generally

    A. direct fear, anger, and other negative emotions against whole groups of people
    B. hold beliefs which are based on insufficient or incorrect information
    C. are fearful and suspicious of things which are different or strange to them
    D. feel that most members of groups believed to be inferior have few attributes in common

12. In terms of its effect on the ability of police to deal effectively with constantly changing situations, the organization structure by itself is generally

    A. *not helpful,* mainly because departmental policies and procedures create obstacles to free and easy operation
    B. *helpful,* mainly because it avoids the necessity of adhering to formal channels of control
    C. *not helpful,* mainly because it is often a static, mechanical device which lacks intelligent discretion
    D. *helpful,* mainly because it is capable of adapting to any situation that confronts it

13. Assume that, because of poor communications in a police department, one level of command does not receive certain orders and directives which other levels do receive. As a result, a bypassed superior officer has no official knowledge of a directive going downward.
    Of the following, the MOST serious consequence of this situation is that the

    A. officer loses control and power over his subordinates
    B. department does not receive the benefit of the officer's services
    C. directive may become outdated before it reaches the officer's attention
    D. officer cannot be held responsible for enforcing the directive

14. Of the following, the ULTIMATE goal of performance evaluation is to

    A. help supervisors recognize weaknesses
    B. improve employee performance
    C. keep employees informed of what is expected of them
    D. verify the accuracy of job descriptions

15. The prevention of individual behavior which would be detrimental to departmental goals is primarily a function of

    A. planning
    B. discipline
    C. counseling
    D. decision-making

16. Assume that a superior officer reduces the number of subordinates he must supervise. As a result of this action, it is MOST likely that

    A. his chain of command will be lengthened
    B. a subordinate's span of control will be narrowed
    C. his chain of command will be shortened
    D. a subordinate's span of control will be broadened

17. Studies of employee motivation show that high group loyalty has an important influence upon performance. The data show that high group loyalty coupled with high production goals in the work group results in high productivity and is generally accompanied by _____ job satisfaction and a feeling of working under_____ pressure.

    A. high; little
    B. high; considerable
    C. low; considerable
    D. low; little

18. Assume that, after a thorough investigation, a superior officer determines that one of his subordinates is guilty of misconduct. The superior officer then tells the subordinate that he wants to speak to him about this matter in a couple of days.
    The superior officer's action in this situation is basically

    A. *wise,* chiefly because it gives the subordinate an opportunity to improve his performance
    B. *unwise,* chiefly because disciplinary action is most effective when taken promptly
    C. *wise,* chiefly because the superior officer has time to consider which form of discipline will be most effective
    D. *unwise,* chiefly because the superior officer may not recall the reasons for the disciplinary action

19. Assume that a small police department allocates 90% of its $500,000 annual budget to personal services and that the average efficiency of personnel is 50%.
    If efficiency could be increased by one-half over its present rate, the amount of wastage of personal budget funds would be reduced to

    A. $112,500   B. $125,000   C. $250,000   D. $337,500

20. One of the most common errors in performance evaluation results from the tendency of the rater to evaluate the subordinate in terms of a general mental attitude toward him rather than by systematic attention to particular traits.
    The one of the following terms which MOST accurately describes this tendency is

    A. leniency
    B. rater bias
    C. contrast error
    D. halo effect

21. In police departments and other organizations, there usually exist both an official organization with its procedures (which are sanctioned by official sources) and an unofficial organization (which is generated by the unofficial will of the group).
    When the official organization and procedures become seriously inconsistent with reality, it is MOST likely that

    A. individual and group behavior will be more rigidly inhibited
    B. the influence of the informal organization will be reduced
    C. the organization chart will be modified to reflect the new situation
    D. unofficial procedure will begin to replace the official for practical purposes

22. Effective dissemination of information is an important aspect of a community relations program. Communication with individuals would generally be more advisable than mass communication EXCEPT when

    A. it is important to observe directly the effect of a message
    B. a message must be spread rapidly to a great many people
    C. the message should reach only those for whom it is specifically intended
    D. it may be necessary to modify a message quickly in order to improve communication

23. The one of the following which is MOST likely to become a major source of friction between police and minority group members is

    A. field interrogation   B. motor scooters
    C. door shaking   D. unmarked patrol cars

24. In order to establish an index of relative need for police services, incidents to which police have allocated patrol time should be classified into all of the following categories EXCEPT

    A. vehicular accidents   B. police hazards
    C. index crimes   D. serving warrants

25. One of the problems that police face in maintaining good community relations is the control of hate groups which preach bigotry. Following are three possible actions that police might take in dealing with such groups:
    I. Insist that the press, radio, and television minimize their coverage of hatemongers and professional agitators
    II. Privately inform city officials and important organizations of the true character and message of the hatemonger
    III. Try to dry up the bigot's sources of income by revealing the involvement of his concealed supporters

    Which of the following choices lists all of the above actions it would generally be ADVISABLE for the police to take?

    A. II, but not I and III   B. I and II, but not III
    C. II and III, but not I   D. I, II, and III

KEY (CORRECT ANSWERS)

1. B
2. D
3. B
4. D
5. C

6. A
7. C
8. D
9. C
10. A

11. D
12. C
13. A
14. B
15. B

16. D
17. B
18. C
19. A
20. D

21. A
22. B
23. C
24. B
25. B

EXAMINATION SECTION
TEST 1

DIRECTIONS: Each question or incomplete statement is followed by several suggested answers or completions. Select the one that BEST answers the question or completes the statement. *PRINT THE LETTER OF THE CORRECT ANSWER IN THE SPACE AT THE RIGHT.*

1. When training your subordinates in a new method of crowd control, which one of the following techniques SHOULD be used?

    A. Teach them the whole job at one time, whether it contains a great many steps or only a few
    B. Issue orders without giving reasons because this will result in more questions and delays
    C. Explain and demonstrate, one step at a time
    D. Use technical language in order to make instructions precise

2. It is sometimes necessary to provide additional training for staff members who are poor in their performance of specific tasks.
Of the following, the MOST effective way of improving staff performance is to

    A. use visual aids along with reading material to train staff on the general subject involved
    B. train subordinates to perform only those tasks which they normally perform
    C. plan and carry out programs to meet the subordinates' real work needs
    D. provide training only for staff members performing critical tasks

3. Assume that as a superior officer you confront one of your subordinate officers with the fact that he is not performing his job effectively. The officer tries to avoid the blame and shifts the criticism to other officers including yourself.
Which one of the following is NOT a good way of handling this situation?

    A. Speaking and acting in an impartial and fair-minded manner
    B. Trying to determine why the officer finds it difficult to accept justifiable criticism
    C. Calling in the other officers whom this subordinate has criticized and having them discuss the matter with him
    D. Listening to the officer, at least at the outset, rather than interrupting his statement

4. For a superior officer to discuss a subordinate's performance evaluation with him is GENERALLY

    A. *inadvisable;* such a discussion will discourage a good worker
    B. *advisable;* the subordinate must know about the quality of his performance for improvement to occur
    C. *inadvisable;* a good performance evaluation will result in the subordinate's asking for more responsibility
    D. *advisable;* such discussions generally lead to a change in the subordinate's evaluation

5. The one of the following which is the MAJOR cause of employee lateness is

   A. low morale
   B. excessive fatigue
   C. accidents
   D. sickness

6. For officers to work together smoothly, teamwork is necessary.
   Which one of the following statements BEST describes the relationship between leadership and teamwork?

   A. Leadership cannot exist without teamwork.
   B. Teamwork cannot exist without leadership.
   C. Leadership and teamwork are one and the same.
   D. There is no relationship between leadership and teamwork.

7. For superiors who wish to achieve proper discipline among subordinates, it is generally MOST difficult to

   A. obtain rapid compliance with orders and directives
   B. prevent subordinates from questioning orders that are issued to them
   C. achieve compliance with orders while encouraging individual initiative
   D. use punishment to prevent infractions of the rules

8. Of the following, it is MOST likely that laxity in administering discipline will result in

   A. a loss of respect for their superior on the part of subordinates
   B. the satisfactory completion of the organization's job
   C. an increase in the number of disturbances at centers
   D. the establishment of proper conditions for successful administration

9. In dealing with a subordinate who shows a lack of interest in performing his duties, a superior officer should GENERALLY

   A. assign to him all the difficult work
   B. give him more responsibility
   C. inspect his performance more often than usual
   D. give him direct, detailed orders

10. A superior officer who has a highly motivated group of officers under his command GENERALLY

    A. shows an interest in how they are doing and is willing to back them up
    B. spends most of his time in closely supervising his subordinates
    C. supervises mainly through one of his subordinate officers
    D. is management-oriented rather than subordinate-oriented

11. As a superior, you might have to supervise subordinate officers who are very enthusiastic and ambitious.
    Which one of the following is the BEST reason for carefully watching the work of such officers?
    They

    A. may produce so much work that other officers resent them
    B. may appear to be overly concerned about being promoted
    C. might make decisions before obtaining the necessary information
    D. may be seeking the superior's job

12. In dealing with the public, officers should behave with courtesy.
    Which one of the following practices would be LEAST effective in promoting courtesy?

    A. Giving advice on subjects about which you are not well informed
    B. Learning to take constructive criticism intelligently
    C. Avoiding discussions of a personal nature
    D. Treating members of the public as you would like to be treated

13. When directing the officers under your command, which one of the following is generally the MOST effective method of supervision?

    A. Provide your directions through written orders to prevent misunderstanding
    B. Supervise every detail of the work closely so that it is carried out exactly as you want it
    C. Limit your concern to getting the job done and not to the people doing the work
    D. Set up general standards and goals so that officers have leeway as to how to achieve them

14. Leadership is particularly important in the security field.
    Of the following, people GENERALLY expect their leader to

    A. state, *Do as I say, not as I do*
    B. refuse to allow changes in orders
    C. get many of his ideas from his subordinates
    D. take his feelings out on those who make mistakes

15. The MOST important single factor in the selection of a person for assignment to a position of greater responsibility should be his

    A. demonstrated ability to do the job
    B. schooling, both civilian and military
    C. training and experience on the job
    D. length of service

16. Security training received by security officers and noted in their personnel charts or records should NOT be used as a basis for

    A. indicating individual degrees of skill
    B. assigning officers to particular shifts
    C. establishing priorities of instruction
    D. presenting a consolidated picture of the training status

17. As a superior officer, you note that one of your subordinates has not been performing his job properly. You discover that the cause of this problem seems to be that he drinks excessively when off duty.
    Of the following, the BEST way to handle this situation is to

    A. discipline the officer to the fullest extent possible
    B. discuss the problem and possible solutions with the officer's fellow workers
    C. wait until the officer has straightened himself out and then counsel him
    D. have a blunt and firm talk with the officer and direct him to seek treatment

18. Officers who are overly sensitive to criticism are one of the problems that superiors must deal with.
    Of the following, which is the BEST way to handle such officers?
    They should

    A. not be talked to differently from other officers
    B. be criticized only on serious mistakes
    C. not be criticized at all
    D. be reassured of their worth to their unit

19. A superior officer who suspects an employee of petty office theft calls the employee to his office and questions him directly.
    In this situation, the superior's action is

    A. *desirable,* primarily because the subordinate should be allowed to answer these accusations privately
    B. *desirable,* primarily because confrontation will persuade the employee to tell the truth
    C. *undesirable,* primarily because line department personnel should handle such matters
    D. *undesirable,* primarily because direct confrontation might unnecessarily embarrass the employee

20. Assume that a certain superior officer assigns a task, without explanation, to a new subordinate who is not yet accepted by the work group.
    Of the following, the MOST likely result of this action would be to

    A. encourage the subordinate to perform at his best
    B. make the subordinate feel insecure about proving himself
    C. stimulate other officers to do their best to impress the new staff member
    D. cause the experienced officers to feel inferior

21. A newly appointed superior officer often faces the problem of supervising officers who were formerly close personal friends of his.
    In this situation, the one of the following which is the BEST approach to take toward these officers is to

    A. break all ties with former friends
    B. stay personally close with friends as this is always an advantage on the job
    C. maintain a relationship of easy, occasional familiarity
    D. become businesslike on the job but remain close socially

22. Assume that you, as a superior officer, are talking over a proposed change in procedure with your subordinates which would require their full cooperation.
    Which one of the following actions would be MOST appropriate for you to take if your subordinates suggest modifications in the procedure?

    A. Prepare arguments against your subordinates' suggestions while you are listening to them
    B. Refuse to accept suggestions for changes since procedures can't be modified
    C. Listen carefully since your subordinates' suggestions may have merit
    D. Accept the recommendations of your more experienced subordinates

23. The successful supervisor should be aware that two of his most important assets are patience and understanding.
Of the following actions by a supervisor, the one that is LEAST likely to demonstrate these qualities would be to

    A. make deadlines realistic and reachable
    B. reprimand an employee the minute he makes a mistake
    C. assist employees in work-related problems
    D. discuss changes in procedures with subordinates

24. One of a supervisor's goals should be to create and maintain a force of loyal subordinates with high morale. This objective is likely to be achieved by all of the following EXCEPT

    A. making subordinate officers feel that their job is an important one
    B. encouraging supervisors to be concerned with the individual needs of subordinates
    C. giving subordinate officers an opportunity to express their thoughts, likes, and interests to their supervisors
    D. having supervisors rely only on the advice of trusted employees when resolving disputes between subordinates

25. One of a supervisor's major responsibilities is to evaluate the performance of his subordinates.
Which one of the following practices would be LEAST productive in developing meaningful evaluations from performance interviews?

    A. Make positive statements only
    B. Outline the points to discuss
    C. Adjust to the individual and situation
    D. Allow the employee to participate

KEY (CORRECT ANSWERS)

1. C
2. C
3. C
4. B
5. A

6. B
7. C
8. A
9. B
10. A

11. C
12. A
13. D
14. C
15. A

16. B
17. D
18. D
19. A
20. B

21. C
22. C
23. B
24. D
25. A

TEST 2

DIRECTIONS: Each question or incomplete statement is followed by several suggested answers or completions. Select the one that BEST answers the question or completes the statement. *PRINT THE LETTER OF THE COREECT ANSWER IN THE SPACE AT THE RIGHT.*

1. Assume that you are a superior officer concerned with improving the attitude of your subordinates toward their work.
   Of the following, the action that is MOST likely to improve this attitude would be for you to

    A. allow your subordinates to take extra time off
    B. interpret rules and regulations leniently
    C. request a merit increase in salary for your subordinates
    D. train your subordinates to perform at the highest possible level

   1.____

2. Assume that two of the officers under your command are hotly disputing the accuracy of a log book entry. One of the officers asks for your opinion.
   Which of the following would be LEAST advisable for you to do in this situation?

    A. Ask the officers to present their views calmly
    B. Keep your temper and remain impartial
    C. Stop the argument and then give your decision
    D. Judge the argument in proportion to its importance

   2.____

3. A superior officer notices that one of his subordinates is not doing his job.
   In this situation, it would be MOST appropriate for the superior officer to

    A. caution the subordinate officer promptly
    B. ignore the incident this time
    C. check on the subordinate officer's behavior in an hour
    D. warn the subordinate officer at the end of his work day that a report may be filed

   3.____

4. A recently appointed superior officer finds it difficult to make the decisions required in his new position.
   Which one of the following suggestions would be MOST helpful to him in overcoming this problem?

    A. Don't be concerned because everyone makes mistakes, and any mistake caused by your decisions will be ignored.
    B. Remember that you will be judged by the long-range soundness of all of your decisions.
    C. Since you are now in charge of a number of officers, let them bear the decision-making responsibility.
    D. Remember that you have a superior and that he can make the decision for you.

   4.____

5. Of the following, the BEST reason for a superior officer to nake inspections and rounds is to

    A. observe the physical appearance of personnel
    B. determine whether communication equipment is working properly

   5.____

41

C. decide whether adequate records are being kept
D. see that the performance of subordinates conforms with departmental standards

6. Assume that you, as a superior officer, have made an inspection and have submitted recommendations for improvements.
Which one of the following actions should be taken to assure that the desired results are obtained from the inspection?
You should

   A. distribute copies of the recommendations to all members of the force
   B. follow-up to determine whether the recommended improvements have been made
   C. give credit to other officers when it is due in order to help increase morale
   D. set up a schedule so that you inspect once a week

7. Assume that you have noticed that one of your subordinates has been quiet and rather depressed for two to three days with no change in his usual satisfactory job performance.
Of the following, the BEST action for you to take in this situation is to

   A. ask him to describe his feelings in detail
   B. act as if you noticed no change in the subordinate's behavior
   C. tell him to forget what's bothering him
   D. recommend that he seek professional guidance

8. Assume that you wish to introduce a change in your subordinates' work procedures in order to improve their performance.
Of the following, the BEST way to gain acceptance of this change is for you to

   A. stress its positive aspects
   B. downgrade past practices
   C. delay discussing it for a while
   D. order your subordinates to follow the new procedure at once

9. Suppose you come across two of your subordinate officers having an argument about the boundaries of their patrol posts.
Which of the following is the LEAST advisable course of action for you to take after stopping the argument?

   A. Tell the officers to speak with you individually
   B. Have the officers submit their views in writing for you to evaluate properly when you have time
   C. Meet with both officers in your office after they finish their tours
   D. Tell the officers to consult you on such matters in the future

10. Assume that a superior officer is explaining a new rule to his men at roll call. One officer states that he does not like the rule. The superior tells the officer that he agrees with him, but that the rule must be followed anyway. In this situation, the superior officer's statement was

    A. *proper*, chiefly because the men should know where superiors stand on rules and regulations
    B. *improper*, chiefly because superiors should not indicate disagreement with a change in rules since they must enforce them

C. *proper,* chiefly because efficiency improves when supervisors and subordinates agree on new rules
D. *improper,* chiefly because questions regarding rule changes should be answered at staff meetings rather than at roll call

11. Assume that you find that several of your subordinate officers have not performed satisfactorily during the last few emergency situations at your work location. The one of the following actions which is LEAST likely to improve their performance is for you to 11.____

    A. keep the subordinates informed about how they performed after each emergency
    B. stay alert for officers who are having difficulty with their work
    C. circulate among the officers at emergencies
    D. avoid the use of criticism

12. Of the following qualifications for an officer, the one that is MOST important is the ability to 12.____

    A. understand and get along with people
    B. write a good report
    C. overcome resistance to arrest
    D. solve crimes

13. Assume that you have noticed that one of your subordinate officers makes errors when questioning clients. You discuss with him the proper method to use when questioning clients. 13.____
    Of the following, your NEXT step should be to

    A. ask another officer to check on your subordinate's procedure when questioning clients
    B. tell the officer to discuss with others how they question clients
    C. have the officer report regularly to you about the clients he questions
    D. watch the officer to see how he questions clients

14. One of the MOST important rules to follow when communicating with your superior is: 14.____

    A. Report everything that happens at your work location to him
    B. Pass on to him rumors and gossip heard within your center
    C. Let him hear from you first about any unusual success, problem or error
    D. Assign to one of your subordinates the responsibility of communicating with your supervisor

15. A superior officer may be required to instruct subordinates in the performance of their tasks. 15.____
    Which of the following would NOT be proper when instructing a small group of employees?

    A. Use simple language
    B. Explain the procedure and the reason for the procedure
    C. Demonstrate one step at a time
    D. Use the lecture method instead of the discussion method whenever possible

16. Assume that a new officer has joined your unit. Which of the following approaches should you, as his superior officer, use in introducing him to the job?

    A. Put him right to work; he will learn best through his mistakes
    B. Act sternly, thereby gaining his respect and indicating the proper supervisor-subordinate relationship
    C. Give him the overall picture of the department and unit he is in
    D. Praise him, even when he makes errors, in order to gain his confidence

17. When a new officer begins work, he will often perform tasks ineffectively, thus requiring corrective action by his supervisor.
    In this situation, which one of the following represents the MOST desirable course of action for the supervisor?

    A. Point out specific errors in performance and how to correct them
    B. Tell the new officer that he is not doing the job properly and assign him to a new task
    C. Avoid criticism in the beginning since it may result in bitterness
    D. Do not criticize because criticism is not currently considered an acceptable tool of management

18. Of the following types of work, the one that is MOST likely to lead to dissatisfaction is work that is

    A. difficult to perform
    B. tiring to complete
    C. uncomplicated
    D. unimportant

19. When instructing subordinates to perform new tasks, the one of the following that is LEAST important in helping then to learn is to

    A. explain the procedure to them in a step-by-step manner
    B. show them what they must do
    C. let them do the task under guidance
    D. have them perform the task without supervision so they may learn from their mistakes

20. Which one of the following is the MOST important single thing to bear in mind about giving orders?

    A. An order should be given to a capable employee, not an uncooperative one.
    B. If an order is given correctly, you will not have to check the work.
    C. An order should be given in as forceful a manner as possible to assure that it is understood.
    D. An order is given because it is necessary to bring about certain results.

21. Suppose that a subordinate asks you about a rumor he has heard. The rumor deals with a subject which your superiors consider *confidential*.
    Which of the following BEST describes how you should answer the officer?
    Tell

    A. the officer that you don't make the rules and that he should speak to higher ranking officers
    B. the officer that you will ask your superior for information

C. him only that you cannot comment on the matter
D. him the rumor is not true

22. Superior officers often find it difficult to *get their message across* when instructing newly appointed officers in their various duties.
The MAIN reason for this is generally that the

    A. duties of the officers have increased
    B. superior officer is often so expert in his area that he fails to see it from the learner's point of view
    C. superior officer adapts his instruction to the slowest learner in the group
    D. new officers are younger, less concerned with job security, and more interested in fringe benefits

23. Assume that you are discussing a security problem with an officer under your command. During the discussion, you see that the officer's eyes are turning away from you and that he is not paying attention.
In order to get the officer's attention, you should FIRST

    A. ask him to look you in the eye
    B. talk to him about sports
    C. tell him he is being very rude
    D. change your tone of voice

24. As a superior officer, you may find it necessary to conduct meetings with your subordinates.
Of the following, which would be MOST helpful in assuring that a meeting accomplishes the purpose for which it was called?

    A. Give notice of the conclusions you would like to reach at the start of the meeting
    B. Delay the start of the meeting until everyone is present
    C. Write down points to be discussed in proper sequence
    D. Make sure everyone is clear on whatever conclusions have been reached and on what must be done after the meeting

25. Every superior officer will occasionally be called upon to deliver a reprimand to a subordinate. If done properly, this can greatly help an officer improve his performance.
Which one of the following is NOT a good practice to follow when giving a reprimand?

    A. Maintain your composure and temper
    B. Reprimand a subordinate in the presence of other officers so they can learn the same lesson
    C. Try to understand why the officer was not able to perform satisfactorily
    D. Let your knowledge of the officer involved determine the exact nature of the reprimand

KEY (CORRECT ANSWERS)

1.	D	11.	D
2.	C	12.	A
3.	A	13.	D
4.	B	14.	C
5.	D	15.	D
6.	B	16.	C
7.	B	17.	A
8.	A	18.	D
9.	B	19.	D
10.	B	20.	D

21. B
22. B
23. D
24. D
25. B

TEST 3

DIRECTIONS: Each question or incomplete statement is followed by several suggested answers or completions. Select the one that BEST answers the question or completes the statement. *PRINT THE LETTER OF THE CORRECT ANSWER IN THE SPACE AT THE RIGHT.*

1. Of the following, the PRIMARY purpose of communications between subordinates and superiors is to

    A. develop language skills
    B. enable subordinates to air their grievances
    C. help establish friendly ties
    D. solve job problems

2. Of the following, the MOST necessary elements of good communication are

    A. openness and form
    B. details and subjectivity
    C. speed and dependability
    D. length and appearance

3. Of the following, the MOST important role of a supervisor is that of

    A. being able to understand how his men feel about their assignments
    B. establishing good contacts with the administration
    C. fulfilling his responsibility to the assigned position
    D. presenting a good public image on the behalf of his organization

4. Of the following, the LEAST desirable behavior of a senior officer would be for him to

    A. attempt to gain the respect of superiors
    B. attempt to find causes of high employee turnover
    C. ignore infrequent latenesses
    D. ignore suggestions which may prove unworthy

5. A senior officer who consults with his subordinates about operational planning is GENERALLY

    A. attempting to prove his supervisory ability
    B. developing their job participation and cooperation
    C. passing down his responsibilities to others
    D. searching for an employee with supervisory ability

6. If a senior officer conducted supervision and inspection programs in order to become aware of his men's conduct, he would GENERALLY be considered to be

    A. excessively strict and authoritarian
    B. looking for potential troublemakers
    C. overconscientious in his work
    D. performing a vital duty

7. Of the following, the BEST reason for a supervisor's evaluation of his own on-the-job performance is to enable him to

    A. find the best methods of supervising his men and in getting the job done
    B. give the impression that he is sincere in trying to become a better supervisor

C. make a favorable impression on his superiors
D. make his work seem more important than it actually is

8. Assume that you are a senior officer making a performance evaluation of an officer. The reason for NOT drawing conclusions too quickly is CHIEFLY that

   A. without due consideration of all the facts, you are likely to evaluate the officer on biased personal judgment
   B. evaluation reports take a great deal of time and thought
   C. senior officers must consult with superiors before drawing conclusions about a subordinate's performance
   D. the officer might try to disprove any wrong information which you may have obtained about him

8.____

9. A senior officer notices two officers, known to be good workers, playing practical jokes and pranks on the other employees.
   In this case, disciplinary action is

   A. *desirable,* chiefly because horseplay on the job is not, strictly speaking, against the rules
   B. *undesirable,* chiefly because good workers tend to correct their own improper actions
   C. *desirable,* chiefly because horseplay could provoke other employees and that would disrupt normal work routine
   D. *undesirable,* chiefly because a supervisor should not get involved with employees' affairs

9.____

10. Resistance to or resentment of training is likely to be an attitude shown by many officers. Therefore, it is important for a senior officer to understand the causes of his men's attitudes and learn how to deal with them. Of the following, which is the BEST method of lessening an officer's resentment of training?

    A. Give the officers extra time off for taking part in the training program
    B. Openly criticize the officer who often makes mistakes during training
    C. Recommend promotions for those who complete the training program quickest
    D. Explain that the purpose of the training is to help them perform their jobs more efficiently

10.____

11. A senior officer required all officers under his supervision to submit a weekly report based on information from their daily log (memo) entries. The senior officer did not examine these reports, but he did file them as proof that the officers were not *sleeping* on the job.
    In general, this practice of the senior officer is considered

    A. *correct,* chiefly because the senior officer has little need of the reports since he is usually on the scene to observe the performance of his men
    B. *incorrect,* chiefly because, if the senior officer asked for reports, he should read or use the information they contain
    C. *correct,* chiefly because any information an officer had could only be based on daily occurrences
    D. *incorrect,* chiefly because the senior officer is placing too much emphasis on accuracy of paper work

11.____

12. Selecting an employee to be trained for performing the supervisor's duties is generally considered

    A. *desirable,* chiefly because it allows the supervisor to avoid many of his duties
    B. *undesirable,* chiefly because it creates the impression that the supervisor is showing favoritism
    C. *desirable,* chiefly because supervisory coverage is assured in the absence of the supervisor
    D. *undesirable,* chiefly because the trainee will cause the supervisor to worry about possible competition and thus neglect the performance of his duties

13. When discussing lateness with an employee, a supervisor should take the employee to an area where the problem can be discussed privately
    Generally, this practice is considered

    A. *desirable,* chiefly because it gives the employee an opportunity to converse with the supervisor in a very casual way
    B. *desirable,* chiefly because it keeps the problem from being discussed in front of an audience
    C. *undesirable,* chiefly because isolating an employee from his co-workers causes the *rumor-mongers* to spread false gossip about the matter
    D. *undesirable,* chiefly because trivial matters can be mentioned in the open without any repercussions

14. When an officer shows a pattern of abuse in his use of sick leave, a senior officer should

    A. ask the officer for medical proof of all future illnesses
    B. discourage other officers from abusing sick leave by giving the offending officer a public warning
    C. interview the officer and inquire about the reasons for his behavior
    D. acknowledge the officer's right to sick leave as set forth in departmental rules and regulations

15. Of the following, the MAJOR reason why grapevines generally develop in an agency is that

    A. employees have too much idle time
    B. employees want to socialize and gossip with other employees while working
    C. superior officers avoid reporting bad news downward from management to subordinates
    D. there is a communication gap between management and employees

16. If a newly-assigned senior officer is doubtful about the exact details of the assignment he is about to give to an officer, he should GENERALLY

    A. ask to speak to the officer in private and give him another assignment
    B. delay giving the assignment until he clears up his own doubt
    C. attempt to explain to the officer what he knows about the assignment in the best possible way
    D. put the assignment in writing

17. Of the following situations, which one would justify a supervisor's giving direct orders to another supervisor's subordinate?

    A. A supervisor away from his normal assignment observes a serious disturbance and gives orders to the officers in that area.
    B. A supervisor foresees a problem that will arise the next day in another district and immediately proceeds to inform the other supervisor's officers of the action they should take.
    C. A supervisor tells an officer under another supervisor to perform a duty a week from today because he feels it is an urgent matter.
    D. None of the above situations would justify direct supervision by any senior officer.

18. In the planning process, which of the following is NOT a recommended practice in preparing your final plan of action?

    A. Obtain all important available facts related to the problem
    B. Clarify the problem before any plan is created
    C. Make the plan easy to understand so that it can be carried out efficiently
    D. Never make assumptions or forecasts about what could occur

19. Of the following, the BEST way for a senior officer to get his subordinates to carry out his orders is to

    A. explain whenever possible why the orders are being given
    B. let subordinates know in advance the penalties for disobeying his orders
    C. describe the steps that must be followed in performing each order
    D. issue all orders in the form of direct and positive commands

20. It is MOST correct to state that race prejudice is to the GREATEST extent

    A. an inborn human characteristic
    B. the result of training and group association
    C. the product of ghetto areas
    D. a condition limited to adults only

21. *Scapegoating* is a form of prejudice which results MAINLY from

    A. degrading minority groups in an effort to secure status for one's own group
    B. shifting the blame for social inadequacies and ills from oneself to others
    C. thinking of people not as individual persons but rather placing them in carelessly formed, all-embracing classifications
    D. maintaining the existing order to prevent other groups from rising in social and economic status

22. The MOST important step in democratic supervision is

    A. allowing the employee a chance to apologize whenever he makes an error
    B. keeping tight control over employees
    C. making the employee realize that he needs your approval in order to keep his position
    D. showing an interest in the welfare of the employee

23. Evaluating a subordinate's likes and dislikes concerning his work is GENERALLY considered to be   23._____

    A. valuable in assigning work details to the subordinate
    B. necessary only when the subordinate complains of dissatisfaction with his daily duties
    C. unnecessary and a waste of time
    D. useful only in establishing a good relationship with the subordinate

24. Employee motivation is very critical in keeping up the morale of employees.   24._____
    Of the following, which is generally the BEST method of supervision which both motivates and maintains high morale?

    A. Aid employees in finding satisfaction in their assignments even if it requires extra time and responsibility
    B. Allow employees to work with a free hand and without daily interruptions
    C. Don't get involved or become concerned with interests or problems of employees outside the job
    D. Prove your friendship to a select number of employees so that the remainder of the staff will feel you are a *good guy* to work for

25. When attempting to motivate an experienced individual, it is BEST for a senior officer to appeal to the person's   25._____

    A. emotions   B. positive interests
    C. negative feelings   D. inhibitions

KEY (CORRECT ANSWERS)

1. D   11. B
2. C   12. C
3. C   13. B
4. D   14. C
5. B   15. D

6. D   16. B
7. A   17. A
8. A   18. D
9. C   19. A
10. D   20. B

21. B
22. D
23. A
24. A
25. B

EXAMINATION SECTION
TEST 1

DIRECTIONS: Each question or incomplete statement is followed by several suggested answers or completions. Select the one that BEST answers the question or completes the statement. *PRINT THE LETTER OF THE CORRECT ANSWER IN THE SPACE AT THE RIGHT.*

1. A police supervisor, while conducting regular staff meetings, has the problem that S, one of his staff, is always very talkative. Although S does make extremely logical and useful contributions to the meetings, he monopolizes too much of the time of the meetings. Which one of the following is the MOST effective approach for the supervisor to use in this case?

    A. In advance, to give S the task of summarizing the major conclusions reached during the meeting
    B. To interrupt S at frequent intervals until he finally *gets the message*
    C. To constantly remind S of the time limitations of the meeting schedule
    D. To remind S that his opinions are worth no more than those of each of the other staff members
    E. To tell S that the purpose of the meeting is not to provide a platform for speech-making

2. An authority on public administration has said, *Good news ascends the hierarchy much more easily than bad news*. Which one of the following is the MOST important reason why this filtering process almost always occurs?

    A. Many a police chief is unbelievably blind as to what is really going on in his agency.
    B. Most police organizations do not want an upward communications system to exist or to work.
    C. Management officials, designing a good upward communications system, deliberately add a filtering process to that system.
    D. Problems are disturbing and subordinates tend to edit upward communications to present a brighter picture than really exists.
    E. Bad news ascending the upward communication channels is generally overstated by subordinates in order to offset the watering down process they know is likely to occur.

3. The *exception principle,* as applied to police supervision, means that a supervisor acts only on those matters coming under his jurisdiction which really require his personal attention.
Which one of the following is the MOST important result of this principle when it is properly implemented?

    A. The supervisor who makes frequent exceptions to policies cannot expect his subordinates to enforce the policies.
    B. The supervisor will not be burdened by performing routine tasks which may properly be disposed of by his subordinates.
    C. The supervisor will be in a better position to observe which of his subordinates perform routine tasks most effectively.
    D. His subordinates will become aware that even seemingly unimportant tasks are, in fact, very important to the proper functioning of the department.

E. His subordinates will more fully understand that effective operation of the department requires that all persons within the department must share equally the burden of performing routine tasks.

4. A captain hears a lieutenant make the following statement to one of his sergeants: *Sergeant, Patrolman P has been out sick a lot recently, and I am very concerned about the staffing problem it has created.*
With which one of the following kinds of sergeants would this order be MOST likely to be effective? A(n)

   A. unreliable sergeant
   B. inexperienced sergeant
   C. experienced, reliable sergeant
   D. antagonist sergeant
   E. sergeant who does everything *by the book*

5. Most authorities in police supervision agree that punishment for similar breaches of conduct should be uniform. Uniformity may involve giving consideration to the conditions under which the infraction occurred and to whether the infraction was intentional or careless or out of lack of knowledge of the rule.
Which one of the following choices BEST evaluates the extent to which *conditions* and *intentions* should be taken into account in maintaining uniformity of penalties?

   A. Both *conditions* and *intentions* should be factors in uniformity.
   B. Neither *conditions* nor *intentions* should be a factor in uniformity.
   C. *Conditions* should be a factor in uniformity but *intentions* should be disregarded.
   D. *Intentions* should be a factor in uniformity but *conditions* should be disregarded.
   E. Authorities generally are unable to draw any consistent rule as to whether or not *conditions* and *intentions* should be factors in uniformity.

6. A patrol sergeant asks his captain to explain to him the scope of that part of his supervisory duties which is known as inspection.
Which one of the following is the BEST answer for the captain to give?

   A. His inspection basically should be limited to thorough and careful investigation of complaints and bad reports.
   B. Basically, his inspection should be limited to operations and procedures and not be concerned with things.
   C. His inspection should basically be limited to results obtained through the work performed by his subordinates.
   D. Since all the patrol programs are carried out by people, his basic focus of inspection should be on people rather than things or procedures.
   E. Everything relating to his part of the police department, including persons, things, procedures, and results, should be included in the scope of his inspection.

7. Which one of the following is the MOST acceptable action that a police captain can take in regard to the delegation of authority?
To

   A. delegate authority for a task which is beyond the capacity of his subordinate to perform
   B. delegate authority only for those tasks which the captain finds distasteful or onerous

C. grant a subordinate a great deal of authority for a certain task at one time and very little authority for the same task at another time
D. permit the subordinate to return the authority to the captain, when the subordinate is reluctant to make a decision he is perfectly capable of making
E. delegate sufficient authority, when he delegates a task, so that the subordinate is able to complete the task

8. A certain authority on police supervision makes both of the following statements on the same page of his text book:
    I. Punishment must be meted out swiftly after detection and proof of the infraction.
    II. An immediate supervisor, discovering misconduct on the part of a subordinate, should allow his emotions to cool before taking punitive action against him.

   Which one of the following inferences in regard to this apparent inconsistency is MOST logically based on the above selection?

   A. Quality of discipline is always more important than speed.
   B. Even an expert may be inconsistent when it comes to taking punitive action.
   C. There is no real inconsistency between the two statements, since the second statement merely balances the speed and effectiveness.
   D. Most employees would rather be penalized immediately, even though in the heat of anger, rather than wait for the penalty until emotions have cooled.
   E. Equity in punishment is so important that the supervisor should not worry about how long an interval has passed when deciding whether a penalty is necessary and, also, what the penalty should be.

9. Which one of the following MOST accurately states the purpose of supervisory inspection?

   A. Solely to catch any patrolman who is violating procedures and regulations
   B. To create a favorable working climate so that patrolmen will voluntarily follow regulations and procedures
   C. To develop the evidence to convict any patrolman who has been found to be violating regulations and procedures
   D. To discover whether tasks are being performed as directed, and whether there are procedural needs which are unmet
   E. Solely to prevent violations of regulations and procedures by an omnipresence which deprives the patrolman of an opportunity for violation

10. A noted police authority writes: In a large precinct, an order issued by the precinct commander is not given directly to the patrolmen but must descend through several levels of authority. This delegation down the chain of command involves no complications but knowledge of the results ascending to the precinct commander only with difficulty.
    Which one of the following choices BEST explains the term *knowledge of the results* as it is used by this authority?

    A. How his order has been issued
    B. That his order has been issued
    C. That his order has been properly executed
    D. What methods were used in executing his order
    E. Whether the order was received by the patrolmen

11. When a formal grievance procedure exists, one of the problems involved is that of possibly having to consider overruling an action of a lower level supervisor. Which one of the following is the BEST rule to apply to this problem?

    A. When the lower level supervisor has made a mistake, it must be corrected.
    B. Even if the lower level supervisor has made a mistake, he should not be overruled under any circumstances.
    C. When a lower level supervisor has made a mistake, it must be corrected, but only after third party arbitration has made a ruling.
    D. Even if the lower level supervisor has made a mistake, he should not be overruled if an acceptable way can be found to justify his mistake.
    E. When a lower level supervisor has made a mistake, it should be corrected, but only if a way can be found to save face for that lower level supervisor.

12. A police commander should be keenly aware of the differences between the formal communication networks of the department (usually written) and the informal communication networks (usually verbal).
    Which one of the following statements concerning informal communications should a police commander recognize as being MOST accurate?

    A. People resent talking about *business* in friendly, after-work discussions.
    B. People often distort verbal communications transmitted through informal channels.
    C. People are usually unwilling to communicate outside of officially designated channels.
    D. Higher levels in the police organization cannot take cognizance of or act on information received informally.
    E. The development of a good formal communication system will eliminate the existence of the informal network.

13. A certain lieutenant is concerned because the morale of a patrolman in his unit has deteriorated and is affecting the quality of his work. With the knowledge of the patrolman's sergeant, he calls the patrolman in for an interview, the purpose of which is to find out what is causing the bad morale. Early in the interview, the patrolman says, *Sergeants don't seem to take the interest in their men they once did.* The lieutenant replies, *As they once did?*
    Which one of the following choices both BEST evaluates the appropriateness of this response and also states the MOST important reason therefor? This response is

    A. *not appropriate,* since it contributes nothing except a *parroting* of the patrolman's statement
    B. *appropriate,* because it is likely to encourage the patrolman to unburden himself
    C. *not appropriate,* because it is not likely to encourage the patrolman in the process of unburdening himself
    D. *not appropriate,* because it fails to elicit a concrete verifiable example of failure by the patrolman's sergeant
    E. *appropriate,* because it will make the patrolman feel that the lieutenant agrees with him and is going to take some corrective action

14. A captain observes that one of his sergeants customarily *does over* a subordinate's work when that subordinate's work is inadequate or unacceptable. The sergeant's reason for this practice is that he sets high standards and requires that all the work of his unit be done well. The captain is evaluating the sergeant.
Which one of the following choices both MOST correctly states whether this sergeant's practice is good or bad and also constitutes the MOST important reason therefor? This practice is

    A. *good,* because it results in the work being done well
    B. *bad,* because it corrodes the initiative and morale of this subordinate
    C. *bad,* because it creates in the man a lack of confidence in the sergeant
    D. *good,* because it sets high standards and requires the man to achieve them
    E. *good,* because it serves as a training device to teach the man by demonstration how to do good work

15. A certain captain is conducting a staff meeting dealing with the inspection function. Sergeants, lieutenants, the planning officer, and the captain's administrative aide are all at the staff meeting. The captain asks then to state the rank or ranks whose duties involve performing the inspection function. Which one of the following is the MOST correct answer?

    A. Only the sergeants have any significant responsibility for performing the inspection function.
    B. Only the lieutenants have any significant responsibility for performing the inspection function.
    C. Only the captain has any significant responsibility for performing the inspection function.
    D. Only the planning officer has any significant responsibility for performing the inspection function.
    E. Sergeants, lieutenants, and the captain all have a responsibility for performing the inspection function.

KEY (CORRECT ANSWERS)

1.	A	6.	E	11.	A
2.	D	7.	E	12.	B
3.	B	8.	C	13.	B
4.	C	9.	D	14.	B
5.	A	10.	C	15.	E

TEST 2

DIRECTIONS: Each question or incomplete statement is followed by several suggested answers or completions. Select the one that BEST answers the question or completes the statement. *PRINT THE LETTER OF THE CORRECT ANSWER IN THE SPACE AT THE RIGHT.*

1. Captain X has a policy of rotating the responsibility for command, in his absence, among three lieutenants with considerably different lengths of seniority. This policy results in a junior lieutenant being given authority over two senior lieutenants on occasion.
Which one of the following both PROPERLY states whether or not this is a sound supervisory procedure and also constitutes the BEST reason therefor? It is

   A. not a sound procedure, since it violates the principle of chain of command
   B. not a sound procedure, since the authority might easily be abused by the junior lieutenant
   C. not a sound procedure, because of the adverse effect on the morale of the senior lieutenants
   D. a sound procedure, since it prevents the senior lieutenants from becoming overly authoritarian
   E. a sound procedure, since this allows all of the lieutenants to exercise command authority under normal operating conditions

1.____

2. In a certain police department, the captain of each precinct has on his staff a position assigned solely to the planning function. In a certain precinct, the captain, in a staff meeting, tells his lieutenants and sergeants that the discovery of needs for planning is part of their supervisory responsibility and that he expects each of then to call to the attention of the planning officer any evidence of need for a plan. At the same time, he tells the planning officer that he, too, shares the responsibility for discovering the need for plans.
Which one of the following BEST states where the final responsibility rests for seeing that plans are developed for existing needs?
With the

   A. captain
   B. sergeants
   C. lieutenants
   D. planning officer
   E. captain, the planning officer, the lieutenants, and the sergeants, jointly

2.____

3. A certain precinct has a staff inspection unit headed by a lieutenant. One of the members of this unit is the reports review officer, a sergeant. His reponsibility is to review reports originating in the precinct for quality control purposes. He finds that a certain report, prepared by a beat patrolman, is lacking certain information.
Which one of the following is the BEST way for him to handle the problem of effecting correction?

   A. To call the report to the attention of his immediate superior, the lieutenant, and let him handle it as he deems best
   B. To take the report directly to the patrolman's sergeant, if this can be done without jeopardizing harmonious working relationships
   C. To bring the report directly to the attention of the patrolman who prepared it, provided that this will not jeopardize harmonious working relationships

3.____

D. Verbally to transmit the information through the chain of command to his lieutenant, to the captain who commands the precinct, and down through the patrol lieutenant and the sergeant
E. In written form, to transmit the information through the chain of command to his lieutenant, to the captain who commands the precinct and down through the patrol lieutenant and the sergeant

4. A police department's informal communication network can be very harmful, but it can also be beneficial to management and to the department generally.
Following are four possible uses of the networks that might be appropriate and beneficial:
   I. Valuable information which a subordinate would not want to communicate officially can be rapidly transmitted to his superior officers through the networks.
   II. Management may use informal communication to clear up the ambiguities of a police operating procedure of importance to the entire department.
   III. A superior officer may use the informal communication networks to give personal advice to a subordinate which he feels he cannot give in his official capacity.
   IV. Management's knowledge of the kind of information being transmitted through the networks can be useful by disclosing subjects as to which formal communications are not functioning as efficiently as they should.

Which one of the following choices lists ALL of the uses of informal communications which are appropriate and beneficial and none which are not?

   A. I, III, and IV are appropriate and beneficial uses, but II is not.
   B. I, II, and IV are appropriate and beneficial uses, but III is not.
   C. II and IV are appropriate and beneficial uses, but I and III are not.
   D. III and IV are appropriate and beneficial uses, but I and II are not.
   E. I and III are appropriate and beneficial uses, but II and IV are not.

5. A certain captain has supervised the three sergeants described below:
   I. Sergeant M, who is known as a strict disciplinarian who often hands out punishment. His men do very good work because they fear the certain and serious consequences of disobedience and poor work.
   II. Sergeant Q, who is definitely not a disciplinarian and rarely hands out punishment. His men do very good work, often beyond what is required or what is expected of them.
   III. Sergeant R, who is known as a disciplinarian, but hands out punishment only occasionally. His men do what is required, because they know that their jobs depend on it, but rarely more.

This captain is classifying his sergeants by their supervisory styles.
Which one of the following choices MOST correctly classifies those sergeants who supervise by leadership and those sergeants who supervise by authority?

   A. I, II, and III all supervise by leadership.
   B. I, II, and III all supervise by authority.
   C. I and III supervise by leadership and II by authority.
   D. II supervises by leadership and I and III by authority.
   E. II and III supervise by leadership and I by authority.

3 (#2)

6. In a certain precinct, the procedure for patrolling a certain trouble location has been the same for many years and is well-known and understood by all men. After an intensive study by staff officers, the precinct commander decides to change this patrol procedure substantially. Since he is concerned about the morale of his men, he is anxious that the order be understood and accepted. Which one of the following techniques will MOST likely obtain the greatest acceptance?

   A. To have the new procedure read at all roll calls and initialed by every patrolman
   B. To explain the basis for the decision to make the change in the written procedure
   C. To issue a carefully written new procedure without any explanation of the basis for the decision to make the change
   D. To call a staff meeting of all of his lieutenants and sergeants and to read the written procedure to them
   E. In issuing a written procedure, to specify a short period for adjustment and to indicate penalties thereafter for failure to accept the procedure

6.____

7. The captain observes that when a patrolman is telling a certain sergeant something, the sergeant often interrupts before the patrolman has completed his message and says, *I know what you are going to say. The answer is no*. Which one of the following choices both is the BEST evaluation the captain should make of this habit of the sergeant and also the MOST important reason for that evaluation?
The habit is

   A. *good,* because the patrolman will come to believe in the sergeant's infallibility
   B. *slightly bad,* but only because it includes an element of discourtesy to the patrolman
   C. *good;* a considerable amount of valuable time can be saved by the sergeant's interruptions
   D. *good;* it helps the sergeant to establish a reputation for being *on top of the job*
   E. *bad;* whether or not the sergeant has understood the message, the patrolman is likely to become discouraged and stop trying to communicate information to the sergeant

7.____

8. A certain district, under the command of Captain M, has been changing ethnically. At the same time, crime rates have risen steadily. Patrolmen in the district, who had always gotten along well with civilians, are experiencing ugly encounters and civilian complaints. Everyone in the district is aware of the problem. The problem reaches a crisis when Captain M is summoned to headquarters for a lengthy meeting. Departmental rumors report that the Captain has been told very strongly that his district must shape up or else. When he returns from the meeting, he says nothing about the meeting but the next day calls a staff meeting of lieutenants and sergeants. Without heat, he tells them that the district has a serious and difficult problem to handle, but that he is confident that, together, they have the brains and leadership to work out the solution. He proceeds to direct a discussion of how to solve the problem.
Which one of the following choices MOST correctly indicates whether this handling of the situation is PROPER and also the BEST reason therefor?
His handling is

   A. *improper,* because he is falsely creating a feeling of calmness and confidence that cannot exist
   B. *proper,* because his calmness and confidence are more likely to help the men solve the problem than any other attitude

8.____

C. *improper,* because he has failed to create in his subordinates the atmosphere of tension which is necessary to stepped-up performance
D. *improper,* because by his calmness and lack of emotion he has failed to convey to his subordinates the full urgency of the situation
E. *proper,* because by his calmness he has created a sense of tension and anxiety in his men which will help them to do a better job of solving the problem

9. A certain police department's records system is organized so that it maintains separate filing systems for criminal incidents (complaints), all other non-criminal incidents (complaints), accidents, and arrested persons. Which one of the following BEST states the MOST appropriate indexing procedure that should be used by this department?

    A. One general alphabetical index for all files
    B. A separate alphabetical index for each of the separate files
    C. One alphabetical index for all incidents (complaints) and a separate index for arrested persons
    D. Separate alphabetical indexes organized by the type of person, i.e., arrestee, victim, witness, suspect
    E. An alphabetical index, covering all criminal incidents (complaints) including arrests, and a separate alphabetical index covering all non-criminal incidents (complaints) including accidents

10. Which one of the following choices, if any, BEST states why it is advisable for large police departments to decentralize their record systems and assign to each operating unit the responsibility for keeping accurate records?

    A. It makes the individual records more usable by the operating units.
    B. It greatly reduces the need for specialized training in record keeping.
    C. It prevents the deliberate distortion of records for work efficiency purposes.
    D. It facilitates bringing together in one place all of the important knowledges on a specific subject.
    E. None of the above is a good reason for decentralizing the record keeping function.

11. A police commander should recognize that discipline is a major function of command. Which one of the following actions is MOST properly recognized as being the true essence of discipline?

    A. Instilling morale through conferences and pep talks
    B. Separating incompetent subordinates from the police service
    C. Requiring subordinates to conform to the policies and procedures of the department
    D. Providing department members with a continuing formal training program
    E. Punishing subordinates for infractions of rules and regulations

12. Modern police organization theory basically has held with the management principle: A narrow span of control is most desirable for efficient operation.
    Which one of the following BEST states another well-established principle which is most directly in contradiction to the span-of-control principle?

    A. Maximum efficiency requires keeping to a minimum the number of supervisory levels in an organization.
    B. There must be rules for carrying out work which will be applied uniformly to all individual cases.

C. There should be a hierarchical arrangement of officers so that each lower office is directly under a higher one.
D. For efficient operation, each police official should be subject to an established norm of conduct and act objectively in his contacts with individuals inside and outside the police department.
E. For efficient operation, the functions of the police department should be differentiated and placed in separate bureaus which are further subdivided into specialized sections or units.

13. In order to *stagger* his shift changes, a certain police commander sets up the following procedure: All men coming to work assigned to even-numbered patrol sectors report to work 15 minutes before the shift change hour, so that they are ready to go on duty on the hour. All on-duty men assigned even-numbered sectors start back to headquarters at 15 minutes before the shift-change hour, so that they are ready to go off duty on the hour. All odd-numbered sector men coming on duty report to work at 15 minutes after the hour, so that they are ready to go on duty 30 minutes after the hour. All odd-numbered sector men on duty start back to the station 15 minutes after the hour, so as to be ready to go off duty 30 minutes after the hour. At the same time, this commander wants to be *fair*, that is, to make sure that all men will still work the same number of hours.
Which one of the following modifications, if any, is MOST necessary to his plan to make it *fair* for all men?

   A. At the same time as men rotate shifts, they should also be rotated between odd-numbered and even-numbered sectors.
   B. At the same time as the men rotate shifts, the type sector (odd or even) required to report early should also be rotated.
   C. If even-numbered sector men report to work early, the odd-numbered sector men should be called in from the field early, and vice versa.
   D. None of the above is necessary, since it is not possible to stagger shift changes without slight discrepancies in hours worked.
   E. None of the above is necessary, since the plan as stated is fair.

14. Recent emphasis on police-community relations has focused attention on the setting of guidelines for police officers to follow in their conversations with citizens. These guidelines relate to conversations mainly in non-arrest situations, although they can include conversations with persons involved in minor violations such as parking and traffic.
Which one of the following suggested guidelines is MOST likely to be appropriate for police officers to follow?

   A. When engaged in a conversation, he has a responsibility for defending the justice of all laws.
   B. He should engage in conversations on subjects involving religious or political ideologies instead of trying to avoid them.
   C. He should spend time conversing with passersby in his patrol area as often as possible in order to convey the friendliness of the police department.
   D. When overhearing conversations uncomplimentary to the police department, he should enter the conversation in order to defend the force.
   E. When engaged in conversation with a citizen, he should try to correct erroneous impressions or information the citizen has about the police department.

15. A certain police commander desires to create effective and workable policies and procedures for the fair and equitable handling of citizen complaints without creating any public fanfare or publicity.
He issues a command-wide general order providing for:
   I. Development of a citizen complaint form so that persons may make complaints without coming in person to the police department
   II. Creation of a position in his own office for the sole purpose of recording complaints and talking to people about their complaints
   III. Strict instructions to all command members to maintain the confidentiality of all complaints, if so requested by complainants
   IV. Procedures for complete investigation of all complaints, including anonymous complaints and telephone calls

Which one of the following BEST states the MOST appropriate criticism of the commander's actions?
His

A. willingness to give credence to anonymous complaints
B. creation of a position whose sole duty is talking to complainants
C. failure to publicize the new procedure to the entire community
D. failure to require that persons make complaints about police officers in person
E. willingness to respect the confidentiality of information that may possibly turn out to be false and vindictive

KEY (CORRECT ANSWERS)

1. E	6. B	11. C
2. A	7. E	12. A
3. B	8. B	13. E
4. A	9. A	14. E
5. D	10. E	15. C

EXAMINATION SECTION
TEST 1

DIRECTIONS: Each question or incomplete statement is followed by several suggested answers or completions. Select the one that *BEST answers* the question or completes the statement. *PRINT THE LETTER OF THE CORRECT ANSWER IN THE SPACE AT THE RIGHT.*

1. Some superior police officers frequently issue orders to subordinates in such a way that it appears to be a request to perform a certain act rather than a direct order to perform it. This practice is GENERALLY

   A. *undesirable,* this method of issuing orders never carries the same weight as a direct command and implies a lack of self-confidence on the part of the superior officer
   B. *desirable,* this method of issuing orders carries almost the same weight as a direct command and is less likely to antagonize subordinates
   C. *undesirable,* this method of issuing orders leaves it up to the subordinate to establish his own priority of performance when several tasks are involved
   D. *desirable,* this method of issuing orders allows the subordinate to determine for himself the precise method of carrying out the order

2. A lieutenant suspects that Sergeant A is supervising Officer B more closely and intensively than seems necessary. For the lieutenant to direct the sergeant in this situation to relax his supervision somewhat would be undesirable MAINLY because

   A. other officers might suspect personal animosity between the sergeant and lieutenant
   B. he may not be fully aware of the facts in the situation
   C. the officer has procedures available for the correction of grievances
   D. such supervision rarely continues for any prolonged period

3. One of the best indications of interest in the job on the part of subordinates is the fact that they ask questions. Such questions are of value CHIEFLY because they

   A. provide an excellent guide to the re-assignment of subordinates
   B. serve to enhance the status of the supervisor when he answers them
   C. indicate the efficiency of the men involved
   D. can be utilized as part of the training process

4. A superior officer is reading orders to a group of officers and observes that one of them appears to be inattentive to the orders being read. This is the first time this officer has appeared to be inattentive. The superior officer thereupon stops reading the orders and asks this officer a question about the orders. The officer responds with an acceptable answer. At this point it would be MOST appropriate for the superior officer to

   A. reprimand the officer severely then and there for his behavior
   B. continue reading the orders since the officer appears to have understood them
   C. continue reading the orders, but plan to surprise the officer at some other time when he is again seemingly inattentive in order to highlight his inattentiveness
   D. emphasize to the group the necessity to be attentive

5. An officer informs the desk officer that he believes that a certain sergeant, whom he mentions by name, is too strict in supervising all the officers, especially when compared with the supervision carried out by the other sergeants in the same command. Of the following, the BEST advice the desk officer can offer this officer is to

   A. suggest that this is a matter that requires a meeting with the captain
   B. remind the officer that the sergeant himself is often subject to severe supervision
   C. tell the officer that acceptance of supervision is a part of his job
   D. tell the officer that he will conduct his own study of the situation

6. A superior officer is newly assigned to a police unit in which a very close personal friend is already assigned as an officer. The superior officer knows that the entire personnel of the unit is generally aware of this close friendship. In this situation, the one of the following actions which would be MOST desirable for the superior officer to take is to

   A. avoid, as much as possible, any conversation with this officer so as not to create any appearance of favoritism
   B. discuss with the officer the ways in which they should conduct themselves so that strict impartiality will prevail
   C. suggest to the officer that he apply for a transfer to a different unit
   D. suspend temporarily and completely his personal friendly relationship with the officer while both are assigned to the same unit

7. One definition of STAFF supervision reads that it is control over the actual function which others are performing, without exercising line command over the persons who are performing the function. This situation arises MOST often in police work

   A. when a uniformed officer is performing a technical or a semi-technical task
   B. in response to police needs at an emergency of considerable magnitude
   C. in response to predictable situations which necessitate the assignment of substantial numbers of men from various commands

8. The police supervisor should realize that the performance of unpleasant duties is GENERALLY

   A. *unavoidable,* it is part of his responsibility as a leader
   B. *undesirable,* they should be avoided whenever possible
   C. *predictable,* mistakes follow an established pattern
   D. *desirable,* the self-discipline required insures supervisory growth

9. After a reprimand of a subordinate for a violation of the rules, the subordinate corrects himself and appears to perform his work acceptably. For the supervisor to remind the subordinate *occasionally* of his past violation would be

   A. *bad,* it suggests that the supervisor is devoting too much time and effort to one individual
   B. *good,* it is an indication of the use of positive discipline on a continuing basis
   C. *bad,* the original corrective action appears to have served its purpose
   D. *good,* the supervisor has the best interests of the subordinate in mind

10. Development and change of practices will characterize public administration during the next twenty years. The public administrator who is taught too specifically what to do may find that his knowledge is not applicable to the situations he eventually must face.
    With this in mind, it would be most logical for the police planner to stress LEAST the

    A. learning process itself
    B. principles of diagnosing situations
    C. basic elements of crime control programs
    D. preparation of more comprehensive procedural manuals

11. The one of the following which is LEAST characteristic of our system of civil rights is that

    A. governmental restrictions on some of these rights are forbidden because there is no constitutional authorization for their restriction
    B. judicial construction of these rights is in a state of change
    C. this system is a product of hundreds of years of political development
    D. this system eliminates the conflict between governmental authority and individual rights

12. Of the following, the one which is the CHIEF barrier to the development of professionalization for police officers throughout the country is the

    A. relatively low entrance requirements for entry into the police field
    B. relatively low salaries paid law enforcement officers despite the hazards that confront them
    C. failure by police administrators to make effective use of the probationary period to eliminate the unfit

13. Police departments have considered it desirable to establish regulations concerning the financial affairs of department members especially with respect to the payment of just debts and the borrowing of money.
    Of the following, the PRINCIPAL reason for these regulations is to

    A. prevent department members from being victimized by unscrupulous money lenders
    B. insure that the morale of department members does not suffer due to excessive borrowing
    C. prevent department members from becoming susceptible to the commission of dishonest acts because of their personal indebtedness
    D. insure that department members intelligently manage their personal financial affairs

14. A superior officer has been newly assigned to desk duty in a patrol precinct. He has noticed that some of the routine reports and forms which are submitted by several subordinate officers are incorrectly filled out.
The one of the following which would be the BEST course of action for the superior officer to follow in this situation would be to

    A. ascertain from the commanding officer whether other superior officers have noticed these same errors and have attempted to correct them
    B. correct these errors himself and also recommend to the commanding officer that all precinct personnel be instructed in the proper completion of forms
    C. inform these subordinate officers as soon as practicable of their errors and what should be done to correct them
    D. wait until additional errors are committed and then use this opportunity to point out how they may be corrected

15. Assume that the suggestion has been made that time clocks be used in station houses to record the hours of reporting for duty by patrolmen.
Of the following, the PRINCIPAL objection to the installation and use of such time clocks is that

    A. a roll call does not completely prevent irregularities in an attendance check
    B. time clocks involve additional clerical work for the station house personnel
    C. time clocks complicate the assignment of patrolmen to posts and details
    D. the present roll call and inspection procedures, which are necessary for other reasons, also provide a check on attendance

16. Assume that a certain lieutenant has developed the practice of handing the sergeants, without comment, brief written notes which are generally concerned with matters of routine operations. Ordinarily, this type of information is given to the sergeants verbally and informally.
The lieutenant's procedure is GENERALLY

    A. *desirable;* the sergeants are less likely to misinterpret such information when it is given in written form
    B. *undesirable;* the lieutenant should take advantage of such opportunities for establishing and maintaining good personal relationships with his subordinates
    C. *desirable;* the lieutenant is able to avoid unnecessary conversation and can devote more time to desk duties
    D. *undesirable;* giving information to subordinates in a written form encourages them to ask many clarifying questions

17. The good supervisor attempts to keep the channels of communication to and from his subordinates generally unobstructed by being open and sincere, even though the subordinates with whom he deals are often somewhat otherwise minded.
With this in mind, a superior officer can BEST achieve fully effective unobstructed two-way communication by

    A. persisting in this behavior and developing the same qualities in his subordinates
    B. playing his role correctly and thereby setting an example
    C. taking immediate strong disciplinary measures
    D. developing mutual interests with his subordinates

18. The standardization of procedures and the proper scheduling of activities in an organization or agency should reduce old-fashioned bossing to a minimum.
    This is so PRIMARILY because

    A. it presupposes the existence of extensive rules and regulations
    B. little doubt should be left in the minds of subordinates as to what they are supposed to do
    C. It is evident that policy makers at the highest level have established reasonable work standards for those at the operating level
    D. the job situation has thus become completely impersonal

18.____

19. A lieutenants who is the commanding officer of a small departmental unit, periodically re-examines the procedures employed in his unit for the purpose of ascertaining whether any procedural changes ought to be made.
    This practice is

    A. *undesirable;* important procedural changes cannot be made solely on the initiative of the lieutenant
    B. *desirable;* the lieutenant is in the best position to immediately institute any procedural changes that he feels are warranted
    C. *undesirable;* the lieutenant should devote all his efforts to the supervision and execution of established procedures
    D. *desirable;* the lieutenant has a responsibility to attempt to improve the operations of his unit

19.____

20. Planning must be continuous at every level and in every unit of the police department even though the general planning job may be the primary concern of one person or bureau.
    The one of the following which is NOT implied by this statement is that such planning

    A. should permeate the entire organization even though it is the first responsibility of the planning officer
    B. should consider the possibility of intradepartmental conflicts arising and the need to eliminate them at lower levels before they develop
    C. is necessary when there is a lack of attention to it at the higher echelons of the department
    D. may stimulate the acceptance of responsibility for effective job performance at all levels in the organization

20.____

KEY (CORRECT ANSWERS)

1.	B	11.	D
2.	B	12.	A
3.	D	13.	C
4.	B	14.	C
5.	D	15.	D
6.	B	16.	B
7.	A	17.	A
8.	A	18.	B
9.	C	19.	D
10.	D	20.	C

TEST 2

DIRECTIONS: Each question or incomplete statement is followed by several suggested answers or completions. Select the one that BEST answers the question or completes the statement. *PRINT THE LETTER OF THE CORRECT ANSWER IN THE SPACE AT THE RIGHT.*

1. The one of the following situations which *BEST* illustrates unity of command in a police organization is when

    A. only one subordinate is directly commanded or supervised by each superior officer
    B. only one superior officer is in complete command of each situation
    C. only one superior officer is responsible for the job performance of subordinate officers
    D. there is a line of command which extends from the lowest to the highest supervisory officers

    1.____

2. The one of the following which, if increased, would MOST likely result in an increased span of control on the part of a supervisory officer is

    A. an intervening period of time required for orders to reach subordinates not actually present
    B. his ability to supervise subordinates effectively
    C. the complexity of the jobs to be performed by subordinates
    D. the effort which must be devoted to extra-departmental conferences and programs

    2.____

3. There is less of a need for specialization of police operations when the overall quality of police personnel is high *MAINLY* because

    A. a greater variety of police tasks can then be successfully performed by the individual patrolman
    B. high quality police personnel frequently possess specialized skills which they have acquired prior to police service
    C. well qualified personnel tend to develop specialized interests and abilities while performing their regular duties
    D. well qualified personnel understand the dangers of overspecialization to a police agency

    3.____

4. The existence of specialized operating units in a police organization is MOST justified when such a unit

    A. assists the patrol force by its use of specialized knowledge and methods
    B. assumes complete and sole responsibility for police performance in a specialized area of activity
    C. devotes an equal amount of time and effort to the duties and responsibilities of the unspecialized patrol force
    D. is relieved of any responsibility for the regular duties of the unspecialized patrol force

    4.____

5. Many supervising police officers complain that they are too often overburdened with an excess of detailed and routine work.
The MOST practical of the following ways available to a supervising police officer to handle such a problem is to

   A. give the highest priority to the completion of this work until satisfactorily accomplished
   B. request at once the assignment of additional and better trained personnel
   C. assign such work to someone who may and can handle it
   D. apportion such work equally among members of the force

6. Objective indexes of police performance, such as crime and accident rates, provide a MOST exact comparison when comparing

   A. *different* police agencies which have similar administrative structures and problems
   B. *different* police agencies which operate in communities which have similar crime problems and are in the same population group
   C. *variations* in efficiency resulting from a change of procedure within a given police department when the change is made in only one procedure and the influence of other factors remains nearly constant
   D. *variations* in efficiency resulting from changes of procedure within a given police department when the comparison is between two successive years and the accuracy of the basic data has been clearly established

7. Crime statistics even when gathered in a scrupulously honest manner and with all due diligence, are *often* unsatisfactory MAINLY because of

   A. the lack of crimes that go unreported
   B. the lack of appropriate statistical formulas
   C. the lack of a system of classification of crimes
   D. incomplete reporting at the level of arrest

8. When internal statistical reports are used for the purpose of making evaluations of unit commands, the one of the following which is LEAST important in preparing these reports is that they

   A. be based upon observations which are true and data which are basically accurate
   B. be ready on the date established for their submission
   C. conform generally to standard directions for their preparation
   D. should reflect favorably on those officers who are making an effort to perform effectively

9. Assume that a nationwide survey reveals that a particular police administrative practice is widely used and that it is quite different from the city practice.
The one of the following which is the MOST reasonable implication of the results of this survey is that the

   A. more widely accepted practice should be instituted in the city on a trial basis immediately
   B. city practice should be evaluated in an effort to determine if it can be improved
   C. city practice should be revised to conform to the more widely accepted practice
   D. police problems of the city are unique and it is unlikely that any administrative changes ought to be made

10. The tasks of coordination, supervision and control are likely to become more complicated as the specialization of a police department increases.
This statement is GENERALLY

   A. *false;* better performance of these tasks is likely to result because of the concentrated attention given to particular police problems
   B. *false;* the proportion of a total force which is specialized is too small to have any effect on these tasks
   C. *true;* the increased number of interrelationships which result from specialization are sources of potential conflict and friction
   D. *true;* the individual specialist resents direction from superior officers who are not themselves specialists

11. The supervisor who is responsible to several superiors is in an advantageous position since he has the benefit of intimate contacts with more people in higher positions.
This statement is GENERALLY

   A. *false,* because a supervisor should not normally be directly responsible to more than one superior at the same time
   B. *true,* since the supervisor is in a position to learn more about the overall operation of the agency
   C. *false,* because there is a tendency in such a case for the supervisor to lose touch with his own subordinates
   D. *true,* since he can sometimes receive more favorable treatment for his subordinates by judicious use of such contacts

12. A large American city requires annual medical examinations of all police personnel. For the police department of the city to adopt such a procedure would be

   A. *undesirable,* chiefly because physical disabilities of an individual can be readily discovered by an examination of records covering absences and sick leave
   B. *undesirable,* chiefly because the police department of the city is uniquely large and such a program would be administratively difficult
   C. *desirable,* chiefly because it would indicate an interest by the department in an area which has a basic relevance to effective police work
   D. *desirable,* chiefly because it would make possible conformance to reasonable and acceptable medical standards of all police personnel involved

13. Assume that the suggestion has been made and adopted that all patrolmen with 20 years or more seniority be permitted to pick their details and assignments, and assume further that a substantial number of these patrolmen do pick *NEW* details or assignments.
The one of the following which would be the *LEAST* serious of the problems created by such a situation would be the

    A. effect on the patrolmen being transferred elsewhere to accommodate these patrolmen with twenty years' service
    B. matter of settling disputes when two or more patrolmen chose the same detail or assignment
    C. possible staffing of certain departmental units with men who are not the most qualified for the work
    D. training required to fit these men for the details and assignments they chose

14. Departmental rules and regulations should try to anticipate all the situations that might arise involving behavior, and should attempt to provide specific rules to cover all such circumstances.
This statement is *GENERALLY*

    A. *true;* the courteous behavior of individual officers is the most important part of a police public relations program
    B. *false;* this will establish minimum standards of courteous behavior and must necessarily discourage the development of much higher standards
    C. *true;* such specific statements in rules and regulations will serve to discourage the making of excuses for discourteous behavior
    D. *false;* there is no practical limit to the possible situations that could be encountered which involve courteous behavior

15. Rumors about critical intergroup tensions should be reported to superior officers by subordinate officers *MAINLY* because

    A. it indicates that the subordinate officers are fulfilling their responsibilities
    B. superior officers are in a better position to assess the danger potential of such rumors
    C. the minority groups affected are thereby more likely to become aware of the sympathetic interest of the police
    D. subordinate officers are the best qualified to recommend remedial action because they are closest to the tensions

16. Gambling is a racket yielding large profits and these profits give a power to the least desirable elements in the community.
The *MOST* dangerous implication for the police of such power is that it

    A. may be used in an attempt to corrupt law enforcement officers
    B. is virtually impossible to check once it gains a foothold in a community
    C. sets a bad example to impressionable youth by exemplifying the fruits of *easy money*
    D. takes advantage of loopholes in the law so as to remain practically immune from the imposition of penalties

17. Over-specialization in youth work by the police is undesirable MAINLY because such over-specialization would lead   17.____

    A. the police to operate in areas and to adopt an approach which is not in line with proper police function
    B. to frequent changes in police programs to meet the variety of individual juvenile problems as they arise
    C. to undesirable competition among the specialized units engaged in youth work
    D. to the condoning of youthful disruptive behavior by the police

18. The decision of the Supreme Court of the United States in the case of *Mallory vs. United States*   18.____

    A. *upheld* a lower court decision which held that promptness of arraignment should be considered in determining the validity of a confession
    B. *reversed* a lower court decision which required that all confidential records of investigative agencies be subject to review by the courts
    C. *upheld* a lower court decision which made admissible as evidence statements elicited during a period of unlawful police detention
    D. *reversed* a lower court decision because the prisoner was not arraigned promptly enough following his arrest

19. The Crime Index of the revised Uniform Crime Reports for the United States includes a crime category called   19.____

    A. aggravated assault   B. larceny under $50
    C. negligent manslaughter   D. statutory rape

20. The one of the following crimes which had the highest clearance rate for the city last year was   20.____

    A. felonies against the person
    B. murder and non-negligent manslaughter
    C. felonies against property
    D. misdemeanors

KEY (CORRECT ANSWERS)

1. B
2. B
3. A
4. A
5. C

6. C
7. A
8. D
9. B
10. C

11. A
12. D
13. B
14. D
15. B

16. A
17. A
18. D
19. A
20. B

———

EXAMINATION SECTION
TEST 1

DIRECTIONS: Each question or incomplete statement is followed by several suggested answers or completions. Select the one that BEST answers the question or completes the statement. *PRINT THE LETTER OF THE CORRECT ANSWER IN THE SPACE AT THE RIGHT.*

1. In an exploration of professionalism and police service, the only attribute of those mentioned which the police officer shares with members of recognized professions involves most police officers'

    A. responsibility to make technical and ethical judgments which affect the client's future
    B. status of high public esteem and respect
    C. affiliation with professionally-oriented organizations
    D. opportunities for mobility in the service
    E. high level of educational requirements

1.____

2. The number of subordinates who can be supervised effectively by one supervisor is the principle of organization known as the *span of control.*
   With regard to police organizations, it would be CORRECT to state that

    A. traditionally, the span of control is broad at the top level and narrow at the lower levels of an organization
    B. as the span of control in an organization is decreased, the number of levels in the chain of command is increased
    C. when delegation of authority is kept to a minimum, the effect is to reduce the span of control
    D. as the quality of training in an organization improves, the span of control should decrease
    E. the type and complexity of work performed in an organization or its subdivisions should not affect the span of control required

2.____

3. The ability to communicate clearly is one of the most important and most neglected supervisory skills.
   Of the following suggested techniques for overcoming barriers to communication with your subordinates, the LEAST appropriate would be to

    A. establish a policy of keeping your subordinates informed as much as possible about matters concerning them
    B. look for *feedback* to determine whether your subordinates understand your communications
    C. consider the personal thoughts and feelings of those with whom you are attempting to communicate
    D. make use of the *grapevine* since information communicated by this means is more readily accepted and understood than information communicated by formal methods
    E. prepare yourself before attempting to communicate by getting ideas clear in your own mind and by determining the objectives you hope to achieve

3.____

4. In general, police organizational structure should provide clear-cut channels of authority. The principle of unity of command reinforces this concept and should not be violated, except in certain cases.
The one of the following exceptions to this principle which is MOST likely to be *unacceptable* is a situation in which a superior officer

   A. assigned to a staff inspection unit exercises authority over subordinate line personnel in conjunction with inspection
   B. exercises authority over subordinate personnel in an emergency in the absence of their regular supervisor
   C. deals directly with subordinates in routine matters, by-passing their immediate superiors
   D. assigned to a communications unit deems it necessary to deal directly with a subordinate who is performing a line function
   E. is assigned to temporarily replace a regular supervisor who is engaged elsewhere

4.____

5. It would be ACCURATE to state that the police *juvenile specialist* should

   A. carry out the patrol and investigative operations concerning juveniles for the entire department
   B. perform preliminary investigation of all juvenile cases to assure gathering of all pertinent data in the case and permit personal contact with the delinquent
   C. become the departmental specialist in community organization and the mobilization of community resources
   D. relieve patrol officers of patrol and inspectional responsibilities concerning juveniles
   E. be constrained by administrative and legal limitations from exercising discretion and making prejudicial disposition of juvenile cases

5.____

6. The use of temporary transfers may be required occasionally as a means of effective coping with staffing difficulties that may arise in the administration of a large police unit. The one of the following which is generally LEAST likely to be a correct statement concerning temporary transfers is that the typical employee involved in temporary transfers may

   A. prefer temporary transfer because it breaks up normal work routines
   B. object to being removed from the social group
   C. feel he is getting an unfair share of disagreeable work
   D. lack training to do the new job
   E. feel the new tasks are not part of his *job description*

6.____

7. Police assignments based on proportionate needs require a careful weighting of factors to reflect the true nature of the problem.
For example, in the expenditure of patrol time, street miles are generally a far more reliable indicator of the need for patrol time than square miles because

   A. square miles do not adequately take into account severe seasonal fluctuations in population
   B. the number of police hazards cannot be accurately determined on a square mile basis
   C. population density factors make square mile computation figures unreliable
   D. high-rise residential developments present special problems
   E. patrol time is involved in going from place to place in performing the many kinds of police activities

7.____

8. Order giving, even in a military or authoritarian environment, should not simply be a matter of dictation to a subordinate, without regard to the effectiveness of the order. The wise police supervisor knows that his orders can be interpreted in three ways – what he actually said, what he thought he said, and what the subordinate thought he said. It can be CORRECTLY concluded from the above statement that the effective police supervisor should

   A. frame most of his orders as requests, because most subordinates resent the authoritarian approach
   B. give orders by command only when emergency situations require direct, immediate action
   C. issue orders in such a manner that the subordinate interprets what he hears in the way the supervisor intended
   D. realize that orders will not be communicated clearly unless they are followed up
   E. give orders in a uniform manner to his subordinates

9. A police officer with command responsibilities should be aware that the hierarchy of authority in which he operates contributes strongly to his problems in supervising others. The one of the following statements which is MOST appropriate concerning supervisory styles in a hierarchical organization is that

   A. supervisors who get general supervision are more likely to practice general supervision themselves
   B. it is difficult for supervisory styles to be handed down from one authority level to another
   C. supervisors who are supervised closely will supervise their subordinates more generally
   D. supervisors who get general supervision are more likely to practice close supervision
   E. good supervision by high level commanders has no perceptible effect on the supervision exercised by lower-level commanders

10. Throughout his career, a certain precinct commander has never varied his approach to handling his command responsibilities. His approach is strictly the *no nonsense* type. He concentrates on keeping units subordinate to him going through specified work routines in highly prescribed ways under continual time pressures.
    Of the following, it would generally be expected that comrianders who carry out their administrative responsibilities on the basis of this concept of management will have units that achieve

    A. high production records more often than not
    B. low production records more often than not
    C. high production about half the time and low production the other half
    D. very stable and predictable but mediocre production records
    E. very unstable, unpredictable, and mediocre production records

11. In conformity with the policy of a newly appointed police commissioner, a commander is about to decentralize many of the command responsibilities in his precinct.
    Of the following, the MOST likely result of this decentralization is that

A. staff units will assume greater control over line functions
B. supervisors will be able to delegate less autonomy to subordinates
C. duplication of specialized staff work will be reduced
D. fewer controls will be needed to keep high-level superiors informed
E. all the operations that should be integrated will come under a common supervisor at a lower level

12. Despite the existence in a police department of a formal communications network, subordinate officers are often confused about orders and directives which have been issued to them.
A commanding officer interested in good communication should be aware of all of the following EXCEPT that

   A. subordinates frequently exaggerate instructions to conform with what they believe their superior officers really want
   B. the same directives will be interpreted in different ways as they are communicated from one organizational level to another
   C. subordinates who are opposed to particular policies will often evade and procrastinate when implementing directives are issued
   D. policy statements that directly affect the individuals involved are generally communicated more accurately than the average directive
   E. the necessity of communicating through formal channels may cause frustrations which lead to bypassing of intermediate levels of command

13. A police captain has received numerous informal complaints about a particular sergeant who works in his precinct. These complaints all center around the fact that the sergeant is too arbitrary and unreasonable in the way he deals with his subordinates. The captain is determined to make this sergeant change his ways for the good of morale in the precinct.
In dealing with behavior-change problems of this kind, the one of the following that is MOST important for the captain to realize is that the

   A. captain must know the motives for the sergeant's behavior in order to change that behavior
   B. sergeant must know the motives for his own behavior before he can change that behavior
   C. sergeant must accept the captain's motivation for trying to change him
   D. sergeant will exert greater control than the captain over how the process turns out
   E. captain will exert greater control than the sergeant over how the process turns out

14. A police lieutenant often feels that his subordinates do not respond to identical job situations in a uniform way because they perceive them differently.
Of the following statements, the one which is generally NOT true of human perception is that people

   A. pay much attention to things that satisfy them
   B. pay little attention to things that satisfy them
   C. tend to distort things that disturb them
   D. ignore things that disturb them
   E. recall satisfying things better than they recall unpleasant things

15. Of the following statements, the one which is NOT characteristic of good disciplinary procedure is that discipline should be

    A. meted out swiftly and related to specific infractions
    B. consistent over time
    C. impersonal and applied to all rule violators
    D. preceded by adequate warnings to those guilty of infractions
    E. applied at unexpected times and in unexpected places to establish its fairness

16. In police supervision, communication is the basic channel by means of which police officers exert influence in directing their subordinates.
    Which of the following statements concerning this superior-subordinate communication process is ACCURATE?

    A. Two-way communication is faster than one-way communication.
    B. One-way communication is more accurate than two-way communication.
    C. In one-way communication, if errors occur, the receiver and sender share in the blame.
    D. One-way communication creates psychological comfort in the sender because he has personal control over how his receivers read him.
    E. Two-way communication permits the receivers to make better judgments of how right or wrong they are concerning their reading of the sender's message.

17. Police officers with command responsibilities should recognize that the practice of delegating authority to subordinate officers rests on an important and basic assumption.
    Which of the following states that assumption ACCURATELY?

    A. Authority can help people who have more of it to structure the behavior of those who have less of it.
    B. All executives supervise better with more of it than with less of it.
    C. The delegation of large quantities of authority to middle and lower ranks is the best guarantee of effective supervision.
    D. The formal authority that is delegated is the sole means by which officers derive their status.
    E. The rank and status of individuals is co-equal with the authority delegated to them.

18. A police lieutenant, in a conference with his commanding officer, is asked to state what he sees as the advantages of using the positional authority conferred on him by his rank.
    Which of his following answers is NOT a valid advantage of such authority?
    It

    A. helps to facilitate coordination and control of his unit
    B. is more simple to deal with persons in his unit on a superior-subordinate basis than it is to deal with them on a man-to-man basis
    C. is an effective agent in changing subordinates' behavior and attitudes in the desired direction
    D. establishes social distance between superior and subordinates and thus insures the positional superiority of the lieutenant
    E. is a fast, efficient way to get things done

19. A police sergeant comments to his superior officer that *the only way to get and keep patrolmen on the ball is to throw the book at them whenever they do something wrong.* This sergeant's view of how to motivate one's subordinates is

A. *appropriate,* chiefly because it still applies to the vast majority of people who work for a living today
B. *inappropriate,* chiefly because it no longer applies to anyone who works for a living
C. *appropriate,* chiefly because it places total emphasis on motivating people on the pull of forces outside the people themselves
D. *inappropriate,* chiefly because supervisors should place greatest emphasis on the push of forces from within people rather than the pull of forces from outside of people
E. *appropriate,* chiefly because it places total emphasis on motivating people on the push of forces inside the people themselves

20. A precinct commander is about to announce a sweeping new departmental directive issued by headquarters. This directive will require everyone subordinate to him – officers and patrolmen – to change their standard operational procedures quite drastically.
Of the following statements, the one which generally is MOST accurate with regard to what this commander can expect when he makes this announcement is that

    A. the non-management personnel will resist the change more strongly than the management personnel
    B. resistance to change can be expected to be as serious in such situations among managers as it is in the ranks of their subordinates
    C. the management personnel will resist the change more strongly than the non-management personnel
    D. little or no resistance will develop as long as the change is not perceived as threatening job security
    E. once the change is understood intellectually by those affected by it, its acceptance and implementation will follow directly

21. In discussing the authoritarian approach to handling people, a tough but well-respected police captain cites a number of advantages to using such an approach.
The one of the statements below which does NOT represent a TRUE advantage of the authoritarian approach to supervising others is that it

    A. facilitates the coordination and control of subordinates and their activities
    B. insures that when it is necessary to do so, a supervisor can use rewards instead of penalties more easily and with greater effect on subordinates
    C. simplifies the supervision of subordinates in the performance of their assigned duties
    D. imposes orderliness and conformity upon diverse activities and large numbers of people
    E. helps to build the self-confidence and capability of the supervisor himself

22. The one of the following statements which is CORRECT concerning the accuracy of police commanders in the evaluation and rating of the productivity of their subordinate officers and their work units is that productivity ratings

    A. are more likely to be accurate when based on the judgment of superiors
    B. are more likely to be inaccurate when based on the judgment of superiors and objective performance criteria
    C. are more likely to be accurate when based on objective judgment and subjective performance criteria

D. based on superiors' judgment are inaccurate when the rating is based less on actual productivity and more on the superiors' perception of how the unit should be managed
E. based on superiors' judgment are inaccurate when the rating is based more on actual productivity and less on the superiors' perception of how the unit should be managed

23. A newly promoted captain has two lieutenants immediately subordinate to him. During his initial interview with Lieutenant S, the captain learns that he gives first priority to the human aspects of his subordinates' problems stating firmly, *The best way to build an effective work team with a high performance record is to let people do the job the way they want to, so long as they accomplish their official objectives.* The other officer, Lieutenant T, gives first priority to insuring that his subordinates perform their duties in a very specific way as dictated by policy and designated by him. When interviewed, he states, *This interest-in-people approach may be all right for some people but not for me. I've got to keep pressure on my subordinates for performance and can't really devote much time to showing an interest in them and their problems.*
The one of the following statements that is MOST likely to be accurate concerning the performance of these subordinate units and their relationship with their supervising lieutenants is that

A. there will be no difference between these groups on either their performance or relationship with their lieutenant
B. there will be no consistent difference between these groups on their performance, but only on their relationship with their lieutenant
C. Lieutenant S supervises a unit that respects him and will consistently outperform Lieutenant T's group
D. Lieutenant T supervises a unit that respects him and will consistently outperform Lieutenant S's group
E. the performance record of either group of subordinates is more closely related to day-to-day events than it is to either Lieutenant's supervisory philosophy and practice

24. In a police department reorganization, a captain loses two lieutenants. One lieutenant supervised a high performance unit while the other supervised a low performance unit. The two lieutenants being transferred in as replacements also have very different records and reputations as managers. Lieutenant Y has the reputation of managing high-producing units, while Lieutenant Z has the reputation of managing low-producing units. Of the following courses of action, the one which would generally give the captain the BEST chance of improving the overall performance and productivity of the two units getting new replacement commanders is for him to

A. place Z in charge of the high-producing unit and Y in charge of the low-producing unit
B. place Y in charge of the high-producing unit and Z in charge of the low-producing unit
C. assign Y and Z to the unit they would personally prefer to supervise
D. assign Y to the unit he would personally prefer to supervise and give Z the other assignment
E. assign Z to the unit he would personally prefer to supervise and give Y the other assignment

25. In dealing with his subordinates, a police captain should recognize that the interpersonal communication process is a vital aspect of his managerial responsibility.
Of the following statements, the one which is MOST accurate concerning the interpersonal communication process is that

    A. the most important dimension in this process is the accurate transmission of material from the sender to the receiver of information
    B. the most important dimension in this process is the accurate receipt of material by the receiver of information
    C. the most important dimension in this process is the acceptance of the information by the person receiving it
    D. transmission, comprehension, and acceptance of information are equally important and will offset the effect of distrust between the superior and subordinate to prevent communications failures
    E. transmission, comprehension, and acceptance of information are equally important, but will not offset the effect of distrust between the superior and subordinate in leading to communications failures

25.____

KEY (CORRECT ANSWERS)

1.	A		11.	E
2.	B		12.	D
3.	D		13.	D
4.	C		14.	B
5.	C		15.	E
6.	A		16.	E
7.	E		17.	A
8.	C		18.	C
9.	A		19.	D
10.	B		20.	B

21.	B
22.	D
23.	C
24.	A
25.	E

TEST 2

DIRECTIONS: Each question or incomplete statement is followed by several suggested answers or completions. Select the one that BEST answers the question or completes the statement. *PRINT THE LETTER OF THE CORRECT ANSWER IN THE SPACE AT THE RIGHT.*

1. Following are three statements relating to staff inspection which MIGHT be accurate: 1.____
    I. In addition to producing much of the information needed to plan and direct the police operator, staff inspections help to maintain efficiency and to eliminate undesirable results from poor practices and faulty techniques
    II. A staff inspection should be conducted by those in direct control of the persons and things being inspected, to see that tasks are satisfactorily performed
    III. Information received through staff inspection is usually more reliable because it is less likely to be biased than information received from a person responsible for the condition being reported

   Which of the following choices lists all of the above statements which ARE accurate?

   A. I is an accurate statement, but II and III are not.
   B. I, II, and III are accurate statements.
   C. I and II are accurate statements, but III is not.
   D. I and III are accurate statements, but II is not.
   E. II is an accurate statement, but I and III are not.

2. The commander of a police precinct assumed the direct responsibility for discovery of infractions, as well as disciplinary actions in matters involving personal conduct on or off duty, inattention to duty, loitering in the station, misuse of equipment, failure to follow verbal or written orders or procedures, and quality of work. 2.____
   Which of the following statements concerning this situation is INCORRECT?

   A. The span of control, insofar as the enforcement of disciplinary action is concerned, was as large in scope as the number of persons in the precinct.
   B. The commander's actions are likely to result in improved observations of undesirable behavior.
   C. The commander should take steps to reorganize the precinct so as to narrow the span of control and establish a clear definition of responsibilities.
   D. Bypassing the chain of command by the commander would have the effect of nullifying the authority of subordinate officers because the men would learn that they (the men) were responsible only to the commander.
   E. A practical result of such a policy is that the commander is physically unable to observe all infractions at all times.

3. Task Force Report: The police made several findings concerning the probationary period for police recruits. Following are three statements that might reflect the findings of the report: 3.____
    I. The probationary period in most cities studied is insufficient in length
    II. Administrators are generally unwilling to exercise their power of dismissal
    III. In most departments, hiring authorities have too much latitude for dismissing probationers.

85

Which of the following choices lists ALL of the above statements that are CORRECT, according to the report?

- A. I, but not II and III
- B. I and II, but not III
- C. II, but not I and III
- D. II and III, but not I
- E. I, II, and III

4. At the scene of a burglary, the patrol sergeant of the precinct of occurrence observes a patrolman from the detective burglary squad conducting a routine investigation. Although the detective is following departmental procedure, the sergeant feels that he should assume command since there is no detective superior present. When the sergeant orders the detective to alter his procedure slightly, the patrolman refuses and continues the investigation in his own manner.
Based on the above facts, which of the following choices is MOST consistent with the spirit of the organizational principle *unity of command*?
The action of

- A. the patrolman was correct. The sergeant was not his commanding officer and there was nothing of an emergency nature involved.
- B. the sergeant was correct. As a supervisor, he has the responsibility for training all subordinate officers with whom he has contact.
- C. the patrolman was incorrect. He should have followed the order regardless of his opinion of the sergeant's competence and later complained to his own superior officer.
- D. the sergeant was incorrect. The expertise of a specialist always takes precedence over the authority of a line superior.
- E. both the sergeant and patrolman were correct. The sergeant does, indeed, have a training responsibility. However, *blind* obedience to superiors of other commands is not required, especially when it is evident that those superiors are incompetent to deal with a specialized situation.

5. A police administrator in a department which recently increased in size becomes aware that he is unable to manage the workload of his office. After analyzing the cause of the problem, he realizes that the greater part of his day is spent in conferences with numerous subordinates who report directly to him. In order to alleviate this problem, he reduces the number of subordinates reporting directly to him by grouping his subordinates into subdivisions and appointing a number of deputies to assume command of them.
This action by the administrator is MOST likely to

- A. facilitate upward-downward communication
- B. simplify organizational structure
- C. broaden the administrator's span of control
- D. reduce the number of levels of command
- E. increase the delegation of authority and responsibility

6. In most police departments, the need for a special police unit devoted to delinquency prevention is indicated by the amount and importance of work to be done. According to authorities, the youth division should be a separate division

- A. on a par with the patrol and detective divisions
- B. on a higher level than the patrol and detective divisions
- C. on a lower level than the patrol and detective divisions
- D. above the patrol division but equal to the detective division
- E. above the detective division but equal to the patrol division

7. Police planning requires systematic analysis of certain factors. Following are five steps in the planning process:
    I. Isolation and clarification of the problem
    II. Collection and analysis of pertinent data and opinions
    III. Selection of the most appropriate alternative
    IV. Discovery of the problem
    V. Identification and evaluation of alternatives

   Which of the following choices lists these steps in the MOST appropriate order?

   A. I, II, V, IV, III
   B. V, IV, I, III, II
   C. IV, I, II, V, III
   D. II, IV, I, III, V
   E. I, IV, II, III, V

8. In order to understand group interactions and group processes, police administrators should realize that

   A. parliamentary procedures which eliminate unproductive behavior in groups generally increase the amount of relevant information that is shared
   B. mechanical barriers are probably the most important barriers to communication in human groups
   C. the more orderly a group is, the more efficient it will be in group processes
   D. barriers which prevent the communication of interpersonal feelings generally improve the communication of facts
   E. seemingly irrelevant behavior by group members may represent attempts to satisfy personal needs

9. Because of the nature of the work, the direction of a police force presents certain problems which are not present in most business organizations. Which of the following is LEAST likely to be a problem which illustrates the difference between police and business operations?

   A. Police duties generally fall into a rigid pattern of kind, place, or time.
   B. Several orders must be given to each police subordinate during each tour of duty.
   C. The police force operates in the field, not in the actual and continuous presence of a superior officer.
   D. Information regarding incidents requiring police services is most frequently received at headquarters, and consequently orders for performing such services must come from headquarters.
   E. The aggregate number of commands in police work is larger than that required in directing most business tasks.

10. Whether a certain branch of police service should be specialized depends upon a consideration of several factors.
    In this regard, it would be INCORRECT to state that the need for specialization increases when

    A. certain services must be readily available, even though there is not sufficient work to occupy one man
    B. there is an insufficient amount of work for all officers to maintain certain essential skills
    C. there is an intermittent and irregular need for particular services
    D. the range of abilities among police officers makes it possible for them to perform successfully a great variety of tasks
    E. officers have an uncooperative attitude toward particular tasks

11. Many authorities in the field of management agree that the degree of pressure exerted by supervisors significantly affects the productivity of their subordinates. Police supervisors should be aware of the fact that, of the following statements concerning the relationship between supervisory pressure and productivity, the one that is generally held to be LEAST valid by these authorities is that

    A. there is an inverse relationship between subordinates' feelings that pressure is *unreasonable* and productivity
    B. there is a direct relationship between subordinates' feelings that pressure is *unreasonable* and productivity
    C. feeling a high degree of pressure is associated with low performance
    D. high pressure results in a low degree of confidence and trust in the supervisor
    E. conflict between supervisors and subordinates is associated with low productivity

12. Controlling is considered to rank with planning and directing as a key administrative process. According to generally accepted expert opinion, in the final analysis, control in a large police department must be achieved and assured through the process of

    A. line inspection
    B. authoritative supervision
    C. training and discipline
    D. staff inspection
    E. voluntary compliance

13. A police commander should be keenly aware that people behave as they do on the job because they are trying to satisfy certain needs that exist within themselves. A noted authority has classified these needs into three major categories, and has further established that these needs seem to exist in a priority-ordered way.
    The one of the following which lists the needs that motivate and control on-the-job behavior in the CORRECT order of priority is _____ needs.

    A. physical, social, psychological
    B. social, physical, psychological
    C. psychological, physical, social
    D. social, psychological, physical
    E. physical, psychological, social

14. Authorities who hold that human factors, particularly group interaction factors, are critical to organizational effectiveness also advocate certain measurements as being important indicators of such effectiveness.
    The one of the following which would NOT typically appear on a list of these measurements is the

    A. extent to which trust and confidence exist in such organizations
    B. extent to which the groups are functioning as groups with high group loyalty
    C. cost-effectiveness of the groups
    D. extent to which good communication exists between groups
    E. clarity with which performance goals set both long-and short-run targets

15. Police administrators sometimes tend to regard their subordinates' resistance to changes they institute as essentially irrational behavior.
From the viewpoint of the human relations approach to the management of resistance to change, the one of the following which is probably the best FIRST step an administrator should take in dealing with such resistance is to

    A. inform his subordinates of changes as soon as possible
    B. advise his subordinates that changes are supported by top management
    C. take a firm stand so that subordinates will not expect any revisions of the changes
    D. institute changes slowly to eliminate the endless state of turmoil following sudden change
    E. establish two-way communication with his subordinates concerning the need for change

16. Following are four possible results of specialization in a police department:
    I. The group responsible for a specific task develops high morale and pride in its accomplishment
    II. The administrative functions of coordination, supervision, and control become less complicated
    III. Responsibility for performance of tasks becomes less definite as specialization increases
    IV. There is a reduction of interest among most members of the department in operations that are performed exclusively by specialists

    Which of the following choices lists ALL of the above that are likely to result from specialization?

    A. I and II
    B. I and IV
    C. II and III
    D. I, III, and IV
    E. I, II, III, and IV

17. *Completed staff work* has been defined as the study of a problem and presentation of a solution, by a staff officer, in such form that all that remains to be done on the part of the staff division, or the commander, is to indicate his approval or disapproval of the completed action.
For a commanding officer to require *completed staff work* is GENERALLY considered

    A. *improper;* it exceeds the limitations of delegated authority and undermines the commander's administrative control
    B. *proper;* it relieves the commander of most of his responsibilities, enabling him to limit his personal attention to matters of planning, policy-making, and public speaking
    C. *improper;* planning, policy, and decision-making may involve difficult interdivisional relationships, requiring the commander's full participation in all states of the work
    D. *proper;* its effectiveness in assisting the commander has been well tested in military organizations and in progressive and well-organized police departments
    E. *improper;* it does not provide supporting information justifying the selected alternative and may result in implementation without adequate consideration by the commander

18. A police superior officer who tries to build rapport and break down status barriers in an attempt to put into practice the guidelines established by authorities on the principles of leadership would MOST probably

   A. listen well and urge subordinates to make their points promptly and clearly
   B. set limits on the time allotted to the discussion of ill-structured problems
   C. put forth contributions in the form of indirect hints or hypothetical questions
   D. maintain control over any tendency of the men to get out of hand
   E. rule out group decisions contrary to his leadership style

19. Analysis of group behavior reveals that groups with high peer-group loyalty tend to display a consistently different pattern of relationships from that shown by groups with a low degree of loyalty.
   Members of groups with greater peer loyalty are MORE likely to have

   A. a greater identification with their group and a greater feeling of belonging to it
   B. more friends outside the organization than inside
   C. conflict between members of the work group
   D. poor attitude toward their organizations even though they have group loyalty
   E. higher production but also high degrees of pressure

20. A management training approach which relies on developing empathy and a high degree of interpersonal rapport is GENERALLY called _____ training.

   A. problem simulation
   B. learning theory
   C. multiple management
   D. sensitivity
   E. self-actualization

21. Specialization in the organization of police work has become so common that it is taken for granted. The use of task specialization as a means of increasing output and efficiency, however, has repercussions.
   The one of the following that is NOT generally considered to be an advantage generated by task specialization is the

   A. reduction of training costs
   B. avoidance of time wasted in shifting employees from one job to another
   C. duplication of equipment normally used on a part-time basis
   D. simplification of job controls development
   E. utilization of less-skilled workers

22. For many years, in keeping with a humanitarian philosophy, the proceedings in the juvenile courts have been characterized by a considerable degree of informality and flexibility.
   Several years ago, the matter of the constitutional rights of juveniles in the criminal justice process was fully considered for the FIRST time by the U.S. Supreme Court in the case of

   A. Gault
   B. Gideon
   C. Escobedo
   D. Messiah
   E. Mapp

23. Planning is an administrative obligation that cannot be avoided, but just as the chief supplies his officers with working tools for the accomplishment of their tasks, so good administrative practice places in his hands the necessary tools for discharging this responsibility.
Of the following, the MOST appropriate listing of essential planning tools is

    A. field supervision, employee suggestion programs, performance evaluation
    B. performance evaluation, inspectional devices, staff work
    C. research and analysis, employee suggestion programs, staff work
    D. employee suggestion programs, inspectional devices, performance evaluation
    E. inspectional devices, research and analysis, staff work

24. Staff services of law enforcement agencies are those non-line functions and activities that help develop departmental personnel, assist the departments to perform their basic responsibilities effectively, and provide meaningful internal controls.
By definition, the one of the following which is NOT included in staff services of the law enforcement agency is

    A. organized crime intelligence
    B. internal investigation
    C. public information
    D. planning and inspection
    E. communications and records

25. The *exception principle* specifies that a supervisor acts in exceptional matters requiring his personal attention while delegating routine matters to subordinates for disposition. Administrative experts consider this to be an organizationally sound procedure MAINLY because it

    A. enables the superior to devote more time to planning and creative thinking
    B. facilitates coordination and integration of effort of members of his command
    C. enables subordinates to *learn by doing,* eliminating the need for formal training to perform the particular function
    D. frees the superior of the responsibility for disposing of routine matters in his command
    E. eliminates the organizational requirement to delegate authority commensurate with responsibility

KEY (CORRECT ANSWERS)

1. D
2. B
3. B
4. C
5. E

6. A
7. C
8. E
9. A
10. D

11. B
12. D
13. A
14. C
15. E

16. B
17. D
18. C
19. A
20. D

21. C
22. A
23. E
24. E
25. A

TEST 3

DIRECTIONS: Each question or incomplete statement is followed by several suggested answers or completions. Select the one that BEST answers the question or completes the statement. *PRINT THE LETTER OF THE CORRECT ANSWER IN THE SPACE AT THE RIGHT.*

1. The mark of a really good police supervisor is that he has the ability to draw conclusions, make proper decisions, and stick to his decisions.
   Such conclusions and decisions should be based PRIMARILY on

   A. insight
   B. logic
   C. inference
   D. facts
   E. planning

2. A principal duty of the police supervisor is the training of his subordinates, since the level of their proficiency is directly related to the amount of training they receive. Manpower is the most important and costly of all items in the police budget.
   The MOST reasonable inference to be drawn from this statement is that

   A. the proficiency of police manpower will increase if operations as a whole are taught in the same sequence that will be followed in actual field practice
   B. the supervisor should take advantage of every opportunity which presents itself to improve the performance of his subordinates through the most efficient training methods
   C. one of the greatest spurs to motivation is the recognition of the police officer that his professional growth depends upon his proficiency
   D. the achievement of proficiency is vitally affected by influences that distract, annoy, or frustrate the student
   E. the number of men in the department will be reduced if effective training can improve the learning rate of police officers

3. Following are five statements that may be major purposes of interviews between a police commander and his subordinates:
   I. Giving information
   II. Appraising a police officer's situation
   III. Motivating police officers
   IV. Obtaining information
   V. Helping to solve personal problems
   Which of the following choices lists ALL of the above statements which ARE major purposes of such interviews?

   A. I, II, III, and IV
   B. II, III, and IV
   C. II, IV, and V
   D. III, IV, and V
   E. I, II, III, IV, and V

4. Police departments, like industrial organizations, often have certain common organizational characteristics that directly affect people's behavior.
   These organizations are hierarchical and are GENERALLY depicted in the shape of a

   A. spoked wheel
   B. long spiral coil

C. three-sided solid with a common vertex
D. long, thin cylinder on a thick rectangular base
E. cluster chain

5. The process of inspection is the key to achieving control in the police agency and is carried out by means of *authoritative* and *staff* inspections.
The one of the following statements which BEST describes an aspect of the inspectional process is:

   A. The purpose of the *inspection team* is to uncover conditions which adversely affect police operations and take corrective steps in the form of immediate action and/or recommendations for follow-up action
   B. *Authoritative* inspection is the direct exercise of administrative control by the delegation of authority to a subordinate who will be responsible for determining whether departmental policies and procedures are being effectively carried out
   C. *Authoritative* inspection is sometimes referred to as functional supervision because it is supervision of the function or task and not of the man
   D. *Staff* inspection is inherent in the command function and is exemplified by the sergeant's responsibility for ensuring day-to-day compliance with orders and procedures
   E. The staff inspection function includes the ferreting out of evidence in support of disciplinary action to be taken against members for whom complaints have been received involving their integrity

6. Assume that a police captain who is the commanding officer of a juvenile unit has found that his subordinate officers are not making proper use of referrals of youths and their families to social work and other community agencies. The captain decides to instruct his men in the techniques of making a good referral.
The one of the following which he should NOT recommend to his officers as an effective referral technique is to

   A. stress the common purpose of the police department and the agency in helping the youth and the family solve their problems
   B. explain the functions of the agency so that the youth and the family can clearly understand them and decide whether they want to use such help
   C. indicate to the youth and the family that it is important for them to be willing to work with the agency over a considerable period of time
   D. order the youths and the families to go to the agency so they can better understand the assistance that the agency can provide
   E. telephone the agency when the youth and the family are not in the room to make certain that they would be willing to accept such a case

7. There is a close, positive correlation between organizational effectiveness and the abilities of police supervisors to skillfully apply proven principles of leadership.
Of the following, the MOST reasonable inference to be drawn from this statement is that

   A. leadership qualities are best developed by training and self-discipline
   B. the application of sound leadership principles depends on man and organization serving each other
   C. skillful supervision produces an organization that is free of frustration and conflict

D. effective leadership in police departments is generally learned through trial and error
E. the supervisor who applies leadership principles will generally get greater respect and productivity from subordinates

8. Appraising individual policemen is extremely difficult. Every effort must be made to protect the individual from capricious judgments, and at the same time a searching assay of the officer's value to the department must be continuously carried out.
When developing procedures for rating police personnel, it is INVALID to work on the assumption that

   A. in the final analysis, personnel evaluation has as its sole purpose discovery of those officers best qualified for promotion
   B. appraisal procedures should be kept simple to increase the probability that they will be effective and objective and reliable
   C. some rating is necessary in all units, if only as a stimulus to better supervision by superior officers
   D. accomplishments as well as deficiencies of the persons being evaluated should be reported upon
   E. rating of individual policemen may lead to the detection of deficiencies in existing selection, training, and operating procedures which are in need of improvement

9. In order to combat juvenile delinquency and youth crime, the President's Commission on Law Enforcement recommended the establishment of Youth Services Bureaus in police departments.
According to the Commission, the Youth Services Bureau should be a(n)

   A. in-house police department unit charged with the responsibility for prompt determination and disposition of juvenile cases as to suitability for prejudicial adjustment or juvenile court referral
   B. specialized probation department unit designed to service and supervise juveniles who have been spared commitment to institutional custody by the juvenile court in order to effect and enhance rehabilitation in the community setting
   C. bureau of police juvenile specialists who would be assigned to the investigation of juvenile delinquents and empowered to conduct hearings and impose sanctions as a form of station house adjustment of less serious cases
   D. community based agency concerned with both delinquent and non-delinquent youths and capable of providing youth counseling and development services. Referrals would be received on a non-coercive basis as an alternative to adjudication before the juvenile court
   E. state-supported social welfare agency concerned with the early release of convicted and sentenced youths who were involved in drug-related non-violent crimes to afford them the opportunity for rehabilitation in a non-institutional setting

10. An important part of modern police administration is the creation of appropriately structured field units, such as the patrol and detective divisions. The structure of an organization influences its adaptability, as well as other forms of efficiency.
The MOST reasonable inference to be drawn from this statement is that

   A. individuals are unhappy unless they know precisely who their official superiors are
   B. the mere mechanical fact of structure influences the way individuals perform their work

C. organizations cannot function unless there is a logically constructed chain of command
D. it is the responsibility of an administrator to devise a structure that emphasizes efficiency primarily in terms of speed
E. the principle of unity of command must apply to those who are commanded, as well as to those who command

11. Because police constantly deal with the great human problem of balance between liberty and authority, professionalism in law enforcement has important implications for police-community relations.
Which of the following is LEAST appropriate for a police department that wishes to achieve both professionalization and good community relations?

    A. Professionally motivated law enforcement officers will not ask for public support to continue to perform in the same old way.
    B. The professional officer recognizes that social change has revolutionized the social control function.
    C. All social institutions need a built-in capability to adapt to social change.
    D. Attitude and motivation are two of the hallmarks of the true professional.
    E. Professionalization includes as a goal the development of personal friendship between the policeman and the citizen.

12. Residents of poverty-afflicted neighborhoods are usually most in need of efficient law enforcement, which may not be forthcoming when the police feel they are disliked and misunderstood.
The police are in the best position to take the initiative in overcoming this problem PRIMARILY because

    A. the police are organized and disciplined
    B. bad community feelings create tensions which residents are unable to overcome
    C. minority community leadership is unwilling to assume a conciliatory role
    D. the civil rights laws mandate affirmative police involvement
    E. public apathy is widespread when crime continues to increase

13. The National Institute on Police and Community Relations, held annually since 1955, was designed to foster interprofessional discourse directed at any community problem in which the police and other leadership groups shared a common concern.
The programs sponsored by the National Institute were NOT specifically designed to

    A. encourage police-citizen partnership in the cause of crime prevention
    B. foster cooperative community efforts in problem solving
    C. assist police in overcoming the problems of minority group recruiting in order to meet court-mandated standards
    D. encourage a cooperative relationship between the police and other agencies in the criminal justice system
    E. assist police and other community leaders in understanding the nature and causes of complex problems in people-to-people relationships

14. The President's Commission on Law Enforcement concluded that police-community relations should be recognized as one of the most important functions of any police department serving a substantial minority population.
Which of the following statements is NOT in accord with the Commission's report on community relations programs?

    A. A community relations program is not a public relations program to *sell the police image* to the people.
    B. Community relations is not the exclusive business of specialized units but the business of an entire department from the chief down.
    C. The police must adapt themselves to the rapid changes in patterns of behavior that are taking place in America.
    D. The needs of good community relations and effective law enforcement will be identical at all times.
    E. Improving community relations involves not only instituting programs and changing procedures and practices, but also re-examining fundamental attitudes.

15. Informing the public by means of sound press relations, periodic reports, and department publications is an important police administrative responsibility.
Such reporting is especially important because problems in law enforcement are FREQUENTLY caused by a(n)

    A. distorted image of police activities engendered by popular films and television programs
    B. unethical approach to public information engaged in by certain investigative journalists
    C. tendency in police reporting to emphasize personal accomplishments rather than service to the public
    D. lack of public support arising from citizen misunderstanding of police purposes and methods
    E. inability on the part of top-level police officials to gain a true picture of the operations of their own departments

16. Which of the following is the most fundamental question today in the area of police-community relations?

    A. How can the general public, including any and all groups, be persuaded to respect the police?
    B. What is the most effective and least costly method of generating public support for necessary police improvements?
    C. What is the proper role of the police under contemporary social circumstances in a free society?
    D. How may communications be improved between the police and minority groups?
    E. What are the best methods for implementing police-community programs?

17. Police departments in all communities with a substantial minority group population must vigorously recruit minority group officers.
Any program designed to succeed in this area must begin by

    A. persuading qualified minority group candidates to apply
    B. assigning minority group officers to personnel interviewing boards
    C. increasing the awareness of minority group problems within the police department

D. developing programs to overcome educational deficiencies of minority group candidates
E. relying on referrals from current police officers as a source for qualified recruits

18. Successful police administration invariably rests on a sound foundation of public support. Public support often depends on how well the public is informed. The public can be best informed when the police readily cooperate with the press and information is carried to the public through the local newspapers.
In order to insure ACCURATE coverage of events, the police administrator should

18.____

A. take the people of the community into his confidence, tell them the problems of his department, and what is being done to solve them
B. adopt policies and procedures designed to aid the press, and carefully explain them to all members of the force so that they may assist in carrying out the police purpose
C. establish procedures that will facilitate the collection of news and ensure prompt accessibility by press representatives to all news information from a single central authorized source
D. release all information immediately to the press and rely on the city editors to decide on the basis of their own judgment what should be printed and what should be withheld
E. release daily news bulletins at the same time everyday, simultaneously to all the papers, in order to avoid favoritism and insure accurate and complete fact distribution

19. A captain in command of a detail at the scene of a pending street demonstration involving an emotional political issue is questioned by a sergeant as to the reasons for the demonstration. The captain replies that, *The reasons for the demonstration do not concern you or your men, just do your jobs.*
Which one of the following choices BEST evaluates the appropriateness of this reply? The response is

19.____

A. *appropriate* since the Constitution of the United States guarantees an absolute right to demonstrate on the public streets
B. *not appropriate* since such information should be transmitted before every demonstration, where possible, from every level of command to the patrolmen and detectives who will be policing the demonstration
C. *appropriate* since the sergeant should not have presumed to question a superior
D. *not appropriate* since a sergeant, as a supervisor, is entitled to have all the information concerning a police matter that the captain has
E. *appropriate* since a policeman must give precisely the same treatment to demonstrators supporting causes which he finds personally or politically obnoxious as to those who support a more favored cause

20. In a discussion of guidelines for police action, the President's Commission on Law Enforcement lists several kinds of police activity which demonstrate the difference between discretionary and non-discretionary behavior. Following are four kinds of police behavior listed by the Commission that MIGHT ordinarily be considered discretionary:

20.____

I. The personal conduct of officers on and off duty
II. Ordering a sidewalk gathering to *break it up*
III. Intervening in a domestic dispute
IV. Whether to cooperate with the fire department in a given situation

According to the Commission, which of the following choices lists all of the above kinds of behavior that ARE ordinarily considered discretionary?

- A. I, but not II, III, and IV
- B. I and IV, but not II and III
- C. II and III, but not I and IV
- D. II, III, and IV, but not I
- E. III and IV, but not I and II

21. In discussing relations between the police and the community, the National Advisory Commission on Civil Disorders urged police response to a number of community needs. The one of the following which was NOT included in the Commission's recommendations regarding relations between the police and the community was the need for

    - A. development of community support for law enforcement
    - B. policy guidelines to assist police in areas where police conduct can create tension
    - C. effective mechanisms through which the citizen can have his grievances handled
    - D. change in police operations in the ghetto to ensure proper individual conduct and to eliminate abrasive practices
    - E. full enforcement of all laws in ghetto areas to afford residents greater protection and eliminate the present high sense of insecurity

22. Which of the following is NOT a basic assumption concerning police and community relations programs in recent years?

    - A. Police participating in such programs are interested in the professional development of law enforcement.
    - B. These programs are basically equivalent to authentic educational programs, as opposed to propaganda.
    - C. The goal of law enforcement in a free society is properly the concern of all segments of society, not simply the police.
    - D. These programs sometimes interfere with the fulfillment of other police responsibilities.
    - E. Police participation in community affairs, in a manner appropriate to their function, does not transform the police into *social engineers.*

23. As a result of surveys made by the National Advisory Commission on Civil Disorders of cities in which civil disorders occurred, at least twelve deeply held grievances were identified and ranked into three levels of relative intensity.
Of the following grievances, the one which ranked HIGHEST and in the FIRST level of intensity was

    - A. discriminatory administration of justice
    - B. police practices
    - C. poor recreation facilities and programs
    - D. inadequate housing
    - E. unemployment and underemployment

24. Experienced police officers have been heard to comment that they did not want to participate in programs involving community organizations because *there is too much talk and too little action.*
Of the following, the MOST direct and logical response to a member of the force making such a comment would be that

   A. both the community and police leadership have a responsibility to instruct and involve all citizens in the quest for ordered liberty
   B. control of crime and delinquency is a total community responsibility with the police department as the focal point for mobilizing community action
   C. police and community goals and efforts need to be mutually supportive and unified by common values and action in order to be effective
   D. community policing is a matter of shared responsibility and requires total involvement of all citizens
   E. action does come about slowly through this democratic process but once a decision has been made it will be on the basis of sound reasoning and with the participation of important community groups

25. The responsibility for conducting investigations into allegations of corruption and misconduct that reflect on the character and reputation of a police department usually resides with the internal affairs unit.
Which of the following is LEAST important in developing the confidence of both members of the force and the public in the internal affairs unit?
That

   A. citizen complainants be fully advised of the decisions and actions resulting from investigations
   B. the unit involve itself in all matters involving efficiency since such violations are often indicative of something more serious
   C. the unit be a fact-finding body which is equally as interested in establishing innocence as guilt
   D. citizens be encouraged to report matters openly to the police
   E. there be immediate recording of all complaints or suspect incidents or actions

KEY (CORRECT ANSWERS)

1. D
2. B
3. E
4. C
5. A

6. D
7. E
8. A
9. D
10. B

11. E
12. A
13. C
14. D
15. D

16. C
17. A
18. B
19. B
20. C

21. E
22. D
23. B
24. E
25. B

PHILOSOPHY, PRINCIPLES, PRACTICES, AND TECHNICS OF SUPERVISION, ADMINISTRATION, MANAGEMENT, AND ORGANIZATION

TABLE OF CONTENTS

	Page
MEANING OF SUPERVISION	1
THE OLD AND THE NEW SUPERVISION	1
THE EIGHT (8) BASIC PRINCIPLES OF THE NEW SUPERVISION	1
I. Principle of Responsibility	1
II. Principle of Authority	2
III. Principle of Self-Growth	2
IV. Principle of Individual Worth	2
V. Principle of Creative Leadership	2
VI. Principle of Success and Failure	2
VII. Principle of Science	3
VIII. Principle of Cooperation	3
WHAT IS ADMINISTRATION?	3
I. Practices Commonly Classed as "Supervisory"	3
II. Practices Commonly Classed as "Administrative"	3
III. Practices Commonly Classed as Both "Supervisory" and "Administrative"	4
RESPONSIBILITIES OF THE SUPERVISOR	4
COMPETENCIES OF THE SUPERVISOR	4
THE PROFESSIONAL SUPERVISOR-EMPLOYEE RELATIONSHIP	4
MINI-TEXT IN SUPERVISION, ADMINISTRATION, MANAGEMENT, AND ORGANIZATION	5
I. Brief Highlights	5
A. Levels of Management	6
B. What the Supervisor Must Learn	6
C. A Definition of Supervision	6
D. Elements of the Team Concept	6
E. Principles of Organization	6
F. The Four Important Parts of Every Job	7
G. Principles of Delegation	7
H. Principles of Effective Communications	7
I. Principles of Work Improvement	7
J. Areas of Job Improvement	7
K. Seven Key Points in Making Improvements	8

	L.	Corrective Techniques for Job Improvement	8
	M.	A Planning Checklist	8
	N.	Five Characteristics of Good Directions	9
	O.	Types of Directions	9
	P.	Controls	9
	Q.	Orienting the New Employee	9
	R.	Checklist for Orienting New Employees	9
	S.	Principles of Learning	10
	T.	Causes of Poor Performance	10
	U.	Four Major Steps in On-the-Job Instructions	10
	V.	Employees Want Five Things	10
	W.	Some Don'ts in Regard to Praise	11
	X.	How to Gain Your Workers' Confidence	11
	Y.	Sources of Employee Problems	11
	Z.	The Supervisor's Key to Discipline	11
	AA.	Five Important Processes of Management	12
	BB.	When the Supervisor Fails to Plan	12
	CC.	Fourteen General Principles of Management	12
	DD.	Change	12

II. Brief Topical Summaries — 13
    A. Who/What is the Supervisor? — 13
    B. The Sociology of Work — 13
    C. Principles and Practices of Supervision — 14
    D. Dynamic Leadership — 14
    E. Processes for Solving Problems — 15
    F. Training for Results — 15
    G. Health, Safety, and Accident Prevention — 16
    H. Equal Employment Opportunity — 16
    I. Improving Communications — 16
    J. Self-Development — 17
    K. Teaching and Training — 17
        1. The Teaching Process — 17
            a. Preparation — 17
            b. Presentation — 18
            c. Summary — 18
            d. Application — 18
            e. Evaluation — 18
        2. Teaching Methods — 18
            a. Lecture — 18
            b. Discussion — 18
            c. Demonstration — 19
            d. Performance — 19
            e. Which Method to Use — 19

PHILOSOPHY, PRINCIPLES, PRACTICES, AND TECHNICS
OF
SUPERVISION, ADMINISTRATION, MANAGEMENT, AND ORGANIZATION

MEANING OF SUPERVISION

The extension of the democratic philosophy has been accompanied by an extension in the scope of supervision. Modern leaders and supervisors no longer think of supervision in the narrow sense of being confined chiefly to visiting employees, supplying materials, or rating the staff. They regard supervision as being intimately related to all the concerned agencies of society, they speak of the supervisor's function in terms of "growth," rather than the "improvement" of employees.

This modern concept of supervision may be defined as follows: Supervision is leadership and the development of leadership within groups which are cooperatively engaged in inspection, research, training, guidance, and evaluation.

THE OLD AND THE NEW SUPERVISION

TRADITIONAL
1. Inspection
2. Focused on the employee
3. Visitation
4. Random and haphazard
5. Imposed and authoritarian
6. One person usually

MODERN
1. Study and analysis
2. Focused on aims, materials, methods, supervisors, employees, environment
3. Demonstrations, intervisitation, workshops, directed reading, bulletins, etc.
4. Definitely organized and planned (scientific)
5. Cooperative and democratic
6. Many persons involved (creative)

THE EIGHT (8) BASIC PRINCIPLES OF THE NEW SUPERVISION

I. Principle of Responsibility
   Authority to act and responsibility for acting must be joined.
   A. If you give responsibility, give authority.
   B. Define employee duties clearly.
   C. Protect employees from criticism by others.
   D. Recognize the rights as well as obligations of employees.
   E. Achieve the aims of a democratic society insofar as it is possible within the area of your work.
   F. Establish a situation favorable to training and learning.
   G. Accept ultimate responsibility for everything done in your section, unit, office, division, department.
   H. Good administration and good supervision are inseparable.

II. Principle of Authority
The success of the supervisor is measured by the extent to which the power of authority is not used.
   A. Exercise simplicity and informality in supervision
   B. Use the simplest machinery of supervision
   C. If it is good for the organization as a whole, it is probably justified.
   D. Seldom be arbitrary or authoritative.
   E. Do not base your work on the power of position or of personality.
   F. Permit and encourage the free expression of opinions.

III. Principle of Self-Growth
The success of the supervisor is measured by the extent to which, and the speed with which, he is no longer needed.
   A. Base criticism on principles, not on specifics.
   B. Point out higher activities to employees.
   C. Train for self-thinking by employees to meet new situations.
   D. Stimulate initiative, self-reliance, and individual responsibility
   E. Concentrate on stimulating the growth of employees rather than on removing defects.

IV. Principle of Individual Worth
Respect for the individual is a paramount consideration in supervision.
   A. Be human and sympathetic in dealing with employees.
   B. Don't nag about things to be done.
   C. Recognize the individual differences among employees and seek opportunities to permit best expression of each personality.

V. Principle of Creative Leadership
The best supervision is that which is not apparent to the employee.
   A. Stimulate, don't drive employees to creative action.
   B. Emphasize doing good things.
   C. Encourage employees to do what they do best.
   D. Do not be too greatly concerned with details of subject or method.
   E. Do not be concerned exclusively with immediate problems and activities.
   F. Reveal higher activities and make them both desired and maximally possible.
   G. Determine procedures in the light of each situation but see that these are derived from a sound basic philosophy.
   H. Aid, inspire, and lead so as to liberate the creative spirit latent in all good employees.

VI. Principle of Success and Failure
There are no unsuccessful employees, only unsuccessful supervisors who have failed to give proper leadership.
   A. Adapt suggestions to the capacities, attitudes, and prejudices of employees.
   B. Be gradual, be progressive, be persistent.
   C. Help the employee find the general principle; have the employee apply his own problem to the general principle.
   D. Give adequate appreciation for good work and honest effort.
   E. Anticipate employee difficulties and help to prevent them.
   F. Encourage employees to do the desirable things they will do anyway.
   G. Judge your supervision by the results it secures.

VII. Principle of Science
Successful supervision is scientific, objective, and experimental. It is based on facts, not on prejudices.
   A. Be cumulative in results.
   B. Never divorce your suggestions from the goals of training.
   C. Don't be impatient of results.
   D. Keep all matters on a professional, not a personal, level.
   E. Do not be concerned exclusively with immediate problems and activities.
   F. Use objective means of determining achievement and rating where possible.

VIII. Principle of Cooperation
Supervision is a cooperative enterprise between supervisor and employee.
   A. Begin with conditions as they are.
   B. Ask opinions of all involved when formulating policies.
   C. Organization is as good as its weakest link.
   D. Let employees help to determine policies and department programs.
   E. Be approachable and accessible—physically and mentally.
   F. Develop pleasant social relationships.

WHAT IS ADMINISTRATION

Administration is concerned with providing the environment, the material facilities, and the operational procedures that will promote the maximum growth and development of supervisors and employees. (Organization is an aspect and a concomitant of administration.)

There is no sharp line of demarcation between supervision and administration; these functions are intimately interrelated and, often, overlapping. They are complementary activities.

I. Practices Commonly Classed as "Supervisory"
   A. Conducting employees' conferences
   B. Visiting sections, units, offices, divisions, departments
   C. Arranging for demonstrations
   D. Examining plans
   E. Suggesting professional reading
   F. Interpreting bulletins
   G. Recommending in-service training courses
   H. Encouraging experimentation
   I. Appraising employee morale
   J. Providing for intervisitation

II. Practices Commonly Classified as "Administrative"
   A. Management of the office
   B. Arrangement of schedules for extra duties
   C. Assignment of rooms or areas
   D. Distribution of supplies
   E. Keeping records and reports
   F. Care of audio-visual materials
   G. Keeping inventory records
   H. Checking record cards and books

I. Programming special activities
J. Checking on the attendance and punctuality of employees

III. Practices Commonly Classified as Both "Supervisory" and "Administrative"
   A. Program construction
   B. Testing or evaluating outcomes
   C. Personnel accounting
   D. Ordering instructional materials

RESPONSIBILITIES OF THE SUPERVISOR

A person employed in a supervisory capacity must constantly be able to improve his own efficiency and ability. He represent the employer to the employees and only continuous self-examination can make him a capable supervisor.

Leadership and training are the supervisor's responsibility. An efficient working unit is one in which the employees work with the supervisor. It is his job to bring out the best in his employees. He must always be relaxed, courteous, and calm in his association with his employees. Their feelings are important, and a harsh attitude does not develop the most efficient employees.

COMPETENCES OF THE SUPERVISOR

I. Complete knowledge of the duties and responsibilities of his position.
II. To be able to organize a job, plan ahead, and carry through.
III. To have self-confidence and initiative.
IV. To be able to handle the unexpected situation and make quick decisions.
V. To be able to properly train subordinates in the positions they are best suited for.
VI. To be able to keep good human relations among his subordinates.
VII. To be able to keep good human relations between his subordinates and himself and to earn their respect and trust.

THE PROFESSIONAL SUPERVISOR-EMPLOYEE RELATIONSHIP

There are two kinds of efficiency: one kind is only apparent and is produced in organizations through the exercise of mere discipline; this is but a simulation of the second, or true, efficiency which springs from spontaneous cooperation. If you are a manager, no matter how great or small your responsibility, it is your job, in the final analysis, to create and develop this involuntary cooperation among the people whom you supervise. For, no matter how powerful a combination of money, machines, and materials a company may have, this is a dead and sterile thing without a team of willing, thinking, and articulate people to guide it.

The following 21 points are presented as indicative of the exemplary basic relationship that should exist between supervisor and employee:

1. Each person wants to be liked and respected by his fellow employee and wants to be treated with consideration and respect by his superior.
2. The most competent employee will make an error. However, in a unit where good relations exist between the supervisor and his employees, tenseness and fear do not exist. Thus, errors are not hidden or covered up, and the efficiency of a unit is not impaired.

3. Subordinates resent rules, regulations, or orders that are unreasonable or unexplained.
4. Subordinates are quick to resent unfairness, harshness, injustices, and favoritism.
5. An employee will accept responsibility if he knows that he will be complimented for a job well done, and not too harshly chastised for failure; that his supervisor will check the cause of the failure, and, if it was the supervisor's fault, he will assume the blame therefore. If it was the employee's fault, his supervisor will explain the correct method or means of handling the responsibility.
6. An employee wants to receive credit for a suggestion he has made, that is used. If a suggestion cannot be used, the employee is entitled to an explanation. The supervisor should not say "no" and close the subject.
7. Fear and worry slow up a worker's ability. Poor working environment can impair his physical and mental health. A good supervisor avoids forceful methods, threats, and arguments to get a job done.
8. A forceful supervisor is able to train his employees individually and as a team, and is able to motivate them in the proper channels.
9. A mature supervisor is able to properly evaluate his subordinates and to keep them happy and satisfied.
10. A sensitive supervisor will never patronize his subordinates.
11. A worthy supervisor will respect his employees' confidences.
12. Definite and clear-cut responsibilities should be assigned to each executive.
13. Responsibility should always be coupled with corresponding authority.
14. No change should be made in the scope or responsibilities of a position without a definite understanding to that effect on the part of all persons concerned.
15. No executive or employee, occupying a single position in the organization, should be subject to definite orders from more than one source.
16. Orders should never be given to subordinates over the head of a responsible executive. Rather than do this, the officer in question should be supplanted.
17. Criticisms of subordinates should, whoever possible, be made privately, and in no case should a subordinate be criticized in the presence of executives or employees of equal or lower rank.
18. No dispute or difference between executives or employees as to authority or responsibilities should be considered too trivial for prompt and careful adjudication.
19. Promotions, wage changes, and disciplinary action should always be approved by the executive immediately superior to the one directly responsible.
20. No executive or employee should ever be required, or expected, to be at the same time an assistant to, and critic of, another.
21. Any executive whose work is subject to regular inspection should, wherever practicable, be given the assistance and facilities necessary to enable him to maintain an independent check of the quality of his work.

MINI-TEXT IN SUPERVISION, ADMINISTRATION, MANAGEMENT, AND ORGANIZATION

I. Brief Highlights

Listed concisely and sequentially are major headings and important data in the field for quick recall and review.

A. Levels of Management
Any organization of some size has several levels of management. In terms of a ladder, the levels are:

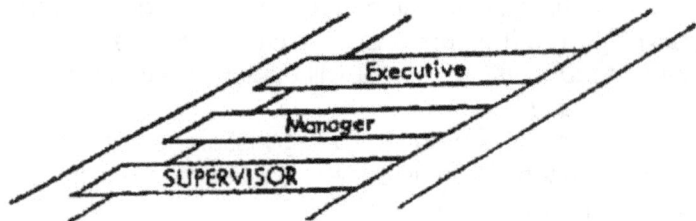

The first level is very important because it is the beginning point of management leadership.

B. What the Supervisor Must Learn
A supervisor must learn to:
1. Deal with people and their differences
2. Get the job done through people
3. Recognize the problems when they exist
4. Overcome obstacles to good performance
5. Evaluate the performance of people
6. Check his own performance in terms of accomplishment

C. A Definition of Supervisor
The term supervisor means any individual having authority, in the interests of the employer, to hire, transfer, suspend, lay-off, recall, promote, discharge, assign, reward, or discipline other employees or responsibility to direct them, or to adjust their grievances, or effectively to recommend such action, if, in connection with the foregoing, exercise of such authority is not of a merely routine or clerical nature but requires the use of independent judgment.

D. Elements of the Team Concept
What is involved in teamwork? The component parts are:
1. Members
2. A leader
3. Goals
4. Plans
5. Cooperation
6. Spirit

E. Principles of Organization
1. A team member must know what his job is.
2. Be sure that the nature and scope of a job are understood.
3. Authority and responsibility should be carefully spelled out.
4. A supervisor should be permitted to make the maximum number of decisions affecting his employees.
5. Employees should report to only one supervisor.
6. A supervisor should direct only as many employees as he can handle effectively.
7. An organization plan should be flexible.

8. Inspection and performance of work should be separate.
9. Organizational problems should receive immediate attention.
10. Assign work in line with ability and experience.

F. The Four Important Parts of Every Job
1. Inherent in every job is the *accountability* for results.
2. A second set of factors in every job is *responsibilities*.
3. Along with duties and responsibilities one must have the *authority* to act within certain limits without obtaining permission to proceed.
4. No job exists in a vacuum. The supervisor is surrounded by key *relationships*.

G. Principles of Delegation
Where work is delegated for the first time, the supervisor should think in terms of these questions:
1. Who is best qualified to do this?
2. Can an employee improve his abilities by doing this?
3. How long should an employee spend on this?
4. Are there any special problems for which he will need guidance?
5. How broad a delegation can I make?

H. Principles of Effective Communications
1. Determine the media.
2. To whom directed?
3. Identification and source authority.
4. Is communication understood?

I. Principles of Work Improvement
1. Most people usually do only the work which is assigned to them.
2. Workers are likely to fit assigned work into the time available to perform it.
3. A good workload usually stimulates output.
4. People usually do their best work when they know that results will be reviewed or inspected.
5. Employees usually feel that someone else is responsible for conditions of work, workplace layout, job methods, type of tools/equipment, and other such factors.
6. Employees are usually defensive about their job security.
7. Employees have natural resistance to change.
8. Employees can support or destroy a supervisor.
9. A supervisor usually earns the respect of his people through his personal example of diligence and efficiency.

J. Areas of Job Improvement
The areas of job improvement are quite numerous, but the most common ones which a supervisor can identify and utilize are:
1. Departmental layout
2. Flow of work
3. Workplace layout
4. Utilization of manpower
5. Work methods
6. Materials handling

7. Utilization
8. Motion economy

K. Seven Key Points in Making Improvements
1. Select the job to be improved
2. Study how it is being done now
3. Question the present method
4. Determine actions to be taken
5. Chart proposed method
6. Get approval and apply
7. Solicit worker participation

L. Corrective Techniques of Job Improvement
Specific Problems
1. Size of workload
2. Inability to meet schedules
3. Strain and fatigue
4. Improper use of men and skills
5. Waste, poor quality, unsafe conditions
6. Bottleneck conditions that hinder output
7. Poor utilization of equipment and machine
8. Efficiency and productivity of labor

General Improvement
1. Departmental layout
2. Flow of work
3. Work plan layout
4. Utilization of manpower
5. Work methods
6. Materials handling
7. Utilization of equipment
8. Motion economy

Corrective Techniques
1. Study with scale model
2. Flow chart study
3. Motion analysis
4. Comparison of units produced to standard allowance
5. Methods analysis
6. Flow chart and equipment study
7. Down time vs. running time
8. Motion analysis

M. A Planning Checklist
1. Objectives
2. Controls
3. Delegations
4. Communications
5. Resources
6. Manpower

7. Equipment
8. Supplies and materials
9. Utilization of time
10. Safety
11. Money
12. Work
13. Timing of improvements

N. Five Characteristics of Good Directions
In order to get results, directions must be:
1. Possible of accomplishment
2. Agreeable with worker interests
3. Related to mission
4. Planned and complete
5. Unmistakably clear

O. Types of Directions
1. Demands or direct orders
2. Requests
3. Suggestion or implication
4. volunteering

P. Controls
A typical listing of the overall areas in which the supervisor should establish controls might be:
1. Manpower
2. Materials
3. Quality of work
4. Quantity of work
5. Time
6. Space
7. Money
8. Methods

Q. Orienting the New Employee
1. Prepare for him
2. Welcome the new employee
3. Orientation for the job
4. Follow-up

R. Checklist for Orienting New Employees   Yes   No
1. Do you appreciate the feelings of new employees when they first report for work?   ___   ___
2. Are you aware of the fact that the new employee must make a big adjustment to his job?   ___   ___
3. Have you given him good reasons for liking the job and the organization?   ___   ___
4. Have you prepared for his first day on the job?   ___   ___
5. Did you welcome him cordially and make him feel needed?   ___   ___

	Yes	No

6. Did you establish rapport with him so that he feels free to talk and discuss matters with you? ___ ___
7. Did you explain his job to him and his relationship to you? ___ ___
8. Does he know that his work will be evaluated periodically on a basis that is fair and objective? ___ ___
9. Did you introduce him to his fellow workers in such a way that they are likely to accept him? ___ ___
10. Does he know what employee benefits he will receive? ___ ___
11. Does he understand the importance of being on the job and what to do if he must leave his duty station? ___ ___
12. Has he been impressed with the importance of accident prevention and safe practice? ___ ___
13. Does he generally know his way around the department? ___ ___
14. Is he under the guidance of a sponsor who will teach the right way of doing things? ___ ___
15. Do you plan to follow-up so that he will continue to adjust successfully to his job? ___ ___

S. Principles of Learning
1. Motivation
2. Demonstration or explanation
3. Practice

T. Causes of Poor Performance
1. Improper training for job
2. Wrong tools
3. Inadequate directions
4. Lack of supervisory follow-up
5. Poor communications
6. Lack of standards of performance
7. Wrong work habits
8. Low morale
9. Other

U. Four Major Steps in On-The-Job Instruction
1. Prepare the worker
2. Present the operation
3. Tryout performance
4. Follow-up

V. Employees Want Five Things
1. Security
2. Opportunity
3. Recognition
4. Inclusion
5. Expression

W. Some Don'ts in Regard to Praise
1. Don't praise a person for something he hasn't done.
2. Don't praise a person unless you can be sincere.
3. Don't be sparing in praise just because your superior withholds it from you.
4. Don't let too much time elapse between good performance and recognition of it

X. How to Gain Your Workers' Confidence
Methods of developing confidence include such things as:
1. Knowing the interests, habits, hobbies of employees
2. Admitting your own inadequacies
3. Sharing and telling of confidence in others
4. Supporting people when they are in trouble
5. Delegating matters that can be well handled
6. Being frank and straightforward about problems and working conditions
7. Encouraging others to bring their problems to you
8. Taking action on problems which impede worker progress

Y. Sources of Employee Problems
On-the-job causes might be such things as:
1. A feeling that favoritism is exercised in assignments
2. Assignment of overtime
3. An undue amount of supervision
4. Changing methods or systems
5. Stealing of ideas or trade secrets
6. Lack of interest in job
7. Threat of reduction in force
8. Ignorance or lack of communications
9. Poor equipment
10. Lack of knowing how supervisor feels toward employee
11. Shift assignments

Off-the-job problems might have to do with:
1. Health
2. Finances
3. Housing
4. Family

Z. The Supervisor's Key to Discipline
There are several key points about discipline which the supervisor should keep in mind:
1. Job discipline is one of the disciplines of life and is directed by the supervisor.
2. It is more important to correct an employee fault than to fix blame for it.
3. Employee performance is affected by problems both on the job and off.
4. Sudden or abrupt changes in behavior can be indications of important employee problems.
5. Problems should be dealt with as soon as possible after they are identified.
6. The attitude of the supervisor may have more to do with solving problems than the techniques of problem solving.
7. Correction of employee behavior should be resorted to only after the supervisor is sure that training or counseling will not be helpful.

8. Be sure to document your disciplinary actions.
9. Make sure that you are disciplining on the basis of facts rather than personal feelings.
10. Take each disciplinary step in order, being careful not to make snap judgments, or decisions based on impatience.

AA. Five Important Processes of Management
1. Planning
2. Organizing
3. Scheduling
4. Controlling
5. Motivating

BB. When the Supervisor Fails to Plan
1. Supervisor creates impression of not knowing his job
2. May lead to excessive overtime
3. Job runs itself—supervisor lacks control
4. Deadlines and appointments missed
5. Parts of the work go undone
6. Work interrupted by emergencies
7. Sets a bad example
8. Uneven workload creates peaks and valleys
9. Too much time on minor details at expense of more important tasks

CC. Fourteen General Principles of Management
1. Division of work
2. Authority and responsibility
3. Discipline
4. Unity of command
5. Unity of direction
6. Subordination of individual interest to general interest
7. Remuneration of personnel
8. Centralization
9. Scalar chain
10. Order
11. Equity
12. Stability of tenure of personnel
13. Initiative
14. Esprit de corps

DD. Change

Bringing about change is perhaps attempted more often, and yet less well understood, than anything else the supervisor does. How do people generally react to change? (People tend to resist change that is imposed upon them by other individuals or circumstances.

Change is characteristic of every situation. It is a part of every real endeavor where the efforts of people are concerned.

1. Why do people resist change?
   People may resist change because of:
   a. Fear of the unknown
   b. Implied criticism
   c. Unpleasant experiences in the past
   d. Fear of loss of status
   e. Threat to the ego
   f. Fear of loss of economic stability

2. How can we best overcome the resistance to change?
   In initiating change, take these steps:
   a. Get ready to sell
   b. Identify sources of help
   c. Anticipate objections
   d. Sell benefits
   e. Listen in depth
   f. Follow up

II. Brief Topical Summaries

   A. Who/What is the Supervisor?
      1. The supervisor is often called the "highest level employee and the lowest level manager."
      2. A supervisor is a member of both management and the work group. He acts as a bridge between the two.
      3. Most problems in supervision are in the area of human relations, or people problems.
      4. Employees expect: Respect, opportunity to learn and to advance, and a sense of belonging, and so forth.
      5. Supervisors are responsible for directing people and organizing work. Planning is of paramount importance.
      6. A position description is a set of duties and responsibilities inherent to a given position.
      7. It is important to keep the position description up-to-date and to provide each employee with his own copy.

   B. The Sociology of Work
      1. People are alike in many ways; however, each individual is unique.
      2. The supervisor is challenged in getting to know employee differences. Acquiring skills in evaluating individuals is an asset.
      3. Maintaining meaningful working relationships in the organization is of great importance.
      4. The supervisor has an obligation to help individuals to develop to their fullest potential.
      5. Job rotation on a planned basis helps to build versatility and to maintain interest and enthusiasm in work groups.
      6. Cross training (job rotation) provides backup skills.

7. The supervisor can help reduce tension by maintaining a sense of humor, providing guidance to employees, and by making reasonable and timely decisions. Employees respond favorably to working under reasonably predictable circumstances.
8. Change is characteristic of all managerial behavior. The supervisor must adjust to changes in procedures, new methods, technological changes, and to a number of new and sometimes challenging situations.
9. To overcome the natural tendency for people to resist change, the supervisor should become more skillful in initiating change.

C. Principles and Practices of Supervision
1. Employees should be required to answer to only one superior.
2. A supervisor can effectively direct only a limited number of employees, depending upon the complexity, variety, and proximity of the jobs involved.
3. The organizational chart presents the organization in graphic form. It reflects lines of authority and responsibility as well as interrelationships of units within the organization.
4. Distribution of work can be improved through an analysis using the "Work Distribution Chart."
5. The "Work Distribution Chart" reflects the division of work within a unit in understandable form.
6. When related tasks are given to an employee, he has a better chance of increasing his skills through training.
7. The individual who is given the responsibility for tasks must also be given the appropriate authority to insure adequate results.
8. The supervisor should delegate repetitive, routine work. Preparation of recurring reports, maintaining leave and attendance records are some examples.
9. Good discipline is essential to good task performance. Discipline is reflected in the actions of employees on the job in the absence of supervision.
10. Disciplinary action may have to be taken when the positive aspects of discipline have failed. Reprimand, warning, and suspension are examples of disciplinary action.
11. If a situation calls for a reprimand, be sure it is deserved and remember it is to be done in private.

D. Dynamic Leadership
1. A style is a personal method or manner of exerting influence.
2. Authoritarian leaders often see themselves as the source of power and authority.
3. The democratic leader often perceives the group as the source of authority and power.
4. Supervisors tend to do better when using the pattern of leadership that is most natural for them.
5. Social scientists suggest that the effective supervisor use the leadership style that best fits the problem or circumstances involved.
6. All four styles—telling, selling, consulting, joining—have their place. Using one does not preclude using the other at another time.

7. The theory X point of view assumes that the average person dislikes work, will avoid it whenever possible, and must be coerced to achieve organizational objectives.
8. The theory Y point of view assumes that the average person considers work to be a natural as play, and, when the individual is committed, he requires little supervision or direction to accomplish desired objectives.
9. The leader's basic assumptions concerning human behavior and human nature affect his actions, decisions, and other managerial practices.
10. Dissatisfaction among employees is often present, but difficult to isolate. The supervisor should seek to weaken dissatisfaction by keeping promises, being sincere and considerate, keeping employees informed, and so forth.
11. Constructive suggestions should be encouraged during the natural progress of the work.

E. Processes for Solving Problems
1. People find their daily tasks more meaningful and satisfying when they can improve them.
2. The causes of problems, or the key factors, are often hidden in the background. Ability to solve problems often involves the ability to isolate them from their backgrounds. There is some substance to the cliché that some persons "can't see the forest for the trees."
3. New procedures are often developed from old ones. Problems should be broken down into manageable parts. New ideas can be adapted from old one.
4. People think differently in problem-solving situations. Using a logical, patterned approach is often useful. One approach found to be useful includes these steps:
   a. Define the problem
   b. Establish objectives
   c. Get the facts
   d. Weigh and decide
   e. Take action
   f. Evaluate action

F. Training for Results
1. Participants respond best when they feel training is important to them.
2. The supervisor has responsibility for the training and development of those who report to him.
3. When training is delegated to others, great care must be exercised to insure the trainer has knowledge, aptitude, and interest for his work as a trainer.
4. Training (learning) of some type goes on continually. The most successful supervisor makes certain the learning contributes in a productive manner to operational goals.
5. New employees are particularly susceptible to training. Older employees facing new job situations require specific training, as well as having need for development and growth opportunities.
6. Training needs require continuous monitoring.
7. The training officer of an agency is a professional with a responsibility to assist supervisors in solving training problems.

8. Many of the self-development steps important to the supervisor's own growth are equally important to the development of peers and subordinates. Knowledge of these is important when the supervisor consults with others on development and growth opportunities.

G. Health, Safety, and Accident Prevention
1. Management-minded supervisors take appropriate measures to assist employees in maintaining health and in assuring safe practices in the work environment.
2. Effective safety training and practices help to avoid injury and accidents.
3. Safety should be a management goal. All infractions of safety which are observed should be corrected without exception.
4. Employees' safety attitude, training and instruction, provision of safe tools and equipment, supervision, and leadership are considered highly important factors which contribute to safety and which can be influenced directly by supervisors.
5. When accidents do occur, they should be investigated promptly for very important reasons, including the fact that information which is gained can be used to prevent accidents in the future.

H. Equal Employment Opportunity
1. The supervisor should endeavor to treat all employees fairly, without regard to religion, race, sex, or national origin.
2. Groups tend to reflect the attitude of the leader. Prejudice can be detected even in very subtle form. Supervisors must strive to create a feeling of mutual respect and confidence in every employee.
3. Complete utilization of all human resources is a national goal. Equitable consideration should be accorded women in the work force, minority-group members, the physically and mentally handicapped, and the older employee. The important question is: "Who can do the job?"
4. Training opportunities, recognition for performance, overtime assignments, promotional opportunities, and all other personnel actions are to be handled on an equitable basis.

I. Improving Communications
1. Communications is achieving understanding between the sender and the receiver of a message. It also means sharing information—the creation of understanding.
2. Communication is basic to all human activity. Words are means of conveying meanings; however, real meanings are in people.
3. There are very practical differences in the effectiveness of one-way, impersonal, and two-way communications. Words spoken face-to-face are better understood. Telephone conversations are effective, but lack the rapport of person-to-person exchanges. The whole person communicates.
4. Cooperation and communication in an organization go hand in hand. When there is a mutual respect between people, spelling out rules and procedures for communicating is unnecessary.
5. There are several barriers to effective communications. These include failure to listen with respect and understanding, lack of skill in feedback, and misinterpreting the meanings of words used by the speaker. It is also common

practice to listen to what we want to hear, and tune out things we do not want to hear.
6. Communication is management's chief problem. The supervisor should accept the challenge to communicate more effectively and to improve interagency and intra-agency communications.
7. The supervisor may often plan for and conduct meetings. The planning phase is critical and may determine the success or the failure of a meeting.
8. Speaking before groups usually requires extra effort. Stage fright may never disappear completely, but it can be controlled.

J. Self-Development
1. Every employee is responsible for his own self-development.
2. Toastmaster and toastmistress clubs offer opportunities to improve skills in oral communications.
3. Planning for one's own self-development is of vital importance. Supervisors know their own strengths and limitations better than anyone else.
4. Many opportunities are open to aid the supervisor in his developmental efforts, including job assignments; training opportunities, both governmental and non-governmental—to include universities and professional conferences and seminars.
5. Programmed instruction offers a means of studying at one's own rate.
6. Where difficulties may arise from a supervisor's being away from his work for training, he may participate in televised home study or correspondence courses to meet his self-development needs.

K. Teaching and Training
1. The Teaching Process
Teaching is encouraging and guiding the learning activities of students toward established goals. In most cases this process consists of five steps: preparation, presentation, summarization, evaluation, and application.

   a. Preparation
   Preparation is two-fold in nature; that of the supervisor and the employee. Preparation by the supervisor is absolutely essential to success. He must know what, when, where, how, and whom he will teach. Some of the factors that should be considered are:
   1) The objectives
   2) The materials needed
   3) The methods to be used
   4) Employee participation
   5) Employee interest
   6) Training aids
   7) Evaluation
   8) Summarization

   Employee preparation consists in preparing the employee to receive the material. Probably the most important single factor in the preparation of the employee is arousing and maintaining his interest. He must know the objectives of the training, why he is there, how the material can be used, and its importance to him.

b. Presentation
In presentation, have a carefully designed plan and follow it. The plan should be accurate and complete, yet flexible enough to meet situations as they arise. The method of presentation will be determined by the particular situation and objectives.

c. Summary
A summary should be made at the end of every training unit and program. In addition, there may be internal summaries depending on the nature of the material being taught. The important thing is that the trainee must always be able to understand how each part of the new material relates to the whole.

d. Application
The supervisor must arrange work so the employee will be given a chance to apply new knowledge or skills while the material is still clear in his mind and interest is high. The trainee does not really know whether he has learned the material until he has been given a chance to apply it. If the material is not applied, it loses most of its value.

e. Evaluation
The purpose of all training is to promote learning. To determine whether the training has been a success or failure, the supervisor must evaluate this learning.
In the broadest sense, evaluation includes all the devices, methods, skills, and techniques used by the supervisor to keep himself and the employees informed as to their progress toward the objectives they are pursuing. The extent to which the employee has mastered the knowledge, skills, and abilities, or changed his attitudes, as determined by the program objectives, is the extent to which instruction has succeeded or failed.
Evaluation should not be confined to the end of the lesson, day, or program but should be used continuously. We shall note later the way this relates to the rest of the teaching process.

2. Teaching Methods
A teaching method is a pattern of identifiable student and instructor activity used in presenting training material.
All supervisors are faced with the problem of deciding which method should be used at a given time.

a. Lecture
The lecture is direct oral presentation of material by the supervisor. The present trend is to place less emphasis on the trainer's activity and more on that of the trainee.

b. Discussion
Teaching by discussion or conference involves using questions and other techniques to arouse interest and focus attention upon certain areas, and by doing so creating a learning situation. This can be one of the most

valuable methods because it gives the employees an opportunity to express their ideas and pool their knowledge.

    c. Demonstration
The demonstration is used to teach how something works or how to do something. It can be used to show a principle or what the results of a series of actions will be. A well-staged demonstration is particularly effective because it shows proper methods of performance in a realistic manner.

    d. Performance
Performance is one of the most fundamental of all learning techniques or teaching methods. The trainee may be able to tell how a specific operation should be performed but he cannot be sure he knows how to perform the operation until he has done so.
As with all methods, there are certain advantages and disadvantages to each method.

    e. Which Method to Use
Moreover, there are other methods and techniques of teaching. It is difficult to use any method without other methods entering into it. In any learning situation, a combination of methods is usually more effective than any one method alone.

Finally, evaluation must be integrated into the other aspects of the teaching-learning process.

It must be used in the motivation of the trainees; it must be used to assist in developing understanding during the training; and it must be related to employee application of the results of training.

This is distinctly the role of the supervisor.